THE COMPLETE UPHOLSTERER

THE COMPLETE UPHOLSTERER

A Practical Guide to Upholstering
Traditional Furniture

Carole Thomerson

FRANCES LINCOLN

FRANCES LINCOLN LIMITED
4 Torriano Mews, Torriano Avenue, London NW5 2RZ

A catalogue record for this book is available from the British Library.

ISBN 0 7112 1092 6

Set in 10 and 11pt Horley Old Style by Bookworm Typesetting, Manchester
Printed in the United States

First Frances Lincoln Edition: November 1989
First Paperback Edition: 1996

4 5 6 7 8 9 10

Illustration from Diderot's Encylopédie

Contents

Introduction

Visits to my grandmother held a particular childhood fascination. I was intrigued by the bobble-fringed, velour-draped mantelpiece and the tinkling cranberry glass. I loved the big black scratchy couch that clanged and creaked. The dining chairs, with their springy carpet-covered seats, stood marshaled around the great square table – extended, with the aid of its polished walnut winding-handle, for high teas which would include fruitcake – dark and delicious – and disgusting jellied eels.

The clanging couch was big enough to roll about on without tipping over backward. The dark wood frames which encircled the deeply buttoned armchair backs glowed rich and shiny; I could draw patterns on the glossy pile of the fabric. There was a tiny dimpled chair which appeared to have no legs but glided and hovered above a long swaying fringe, and there was a wonderful shaped "thing" on which two people could sit back to front – and still face one another.

Of course, it was dreadfully old-fashioned. All the other homes I knew were filling fast with lightweight, spindle-legged contemporary stuff. Sheets of hardboard were being slammed over grainy paneled doors. Marble fireplaces and thickly encrusted ceiling rosettes were being ripped out and dispatched with a shudder of relief: dust traps were gone, easy-wipe was in. I understood that creating a "modern" home was "progress" – and I loved my grandmother's sitting room all the more.

I still have no liking for 1950s furniture, and an old sofa, however shabby, or a buttoned chair, however derelict, is to me a thing of joy. One of my aims in this book is to share my passion for upholstery and to convey the romance, exhilaration, and satisfaction I experience in my work transforming the shabby and the derelict into things of beauty. This includes investigating old upholstery or seating so that as far as possible its original shape, cover, and trimming can be preserved or restored. Sometimes conservation alone is required, when original and often frail upholstery has to be carefully removed for frame repairs and then replaced and strengthened as necessary. My partner and I also create new upholstery. Some of the incredibly exotic 19th-century-revivalist pieces that we produce call for over-the-top treatments which push out the boundaries of shape and technique, offering an antidote to the strict disciplines of conservation and restoration.

Much of our upholstery is simpler, but each piece is always an individual, its character achieved through attention to line, proportion, and detail. The spirit of a chair is conveyed by such subtleties – if it is cushioned, it should be full and fat with feathers; cords should nestle in padding, piping sharpen outlines, gathering and pleating over curves appear casually random but pleasing to the eye. Therefore, a further aim of this book is to describe the *techniques* that upholstery work involves but, while doing so, to convey the thrill of using them to translate one's feelings about the frame into a three-dimensional upholstery form.

The upholstered shape of this late-19th-century tub chair was originally quite plain, but its gentle curves inspired me to translate it to a very different mood. I accentuated the curve of the back and arms with fat corded rolls and echoed the circular shape of the seat in the buttoning pattern. The swells and dips of the pleated tufting and the fullness of the gathered front border create a sensuousness that seems to suggest that the chair is reaching out to embrace the sitter.

This chair is a particular favorite of mine, and I have kept it at muslin stage as a sample to demonstrate to my clients the sumptuous and elaborate shapes that can be achieved.

Upholstery seating is, of course, a highly skilled craft requiring practice, diligent application, and attention to detail. There are rules that must be followed and specific methods for creating the basic shapes. These are detailed in the section on upholstery techniques on pages 64 to 113 and are applied to eight projects on pages 114 to 165, starting with a simple slip seat and progressing to more difficult projects, which should not be undertaken until you have acquired the skills to create the basic shapes. Practice on simple projects to gain technical competence, and as your confidence increases, start to experiment with your frames to create different shapes and moods. If you suspect that a piece you are thinking of upholstering is rare and valuable, or of particular interest, seek expert advice. You may decide to wait until your expertise has increased.

If my book comes anywhere near to achieving its aims, you will be embarking on a life-long relationship with upholstery. Your home (and probably those of your family and friends) will welcome many lovely pieces – and some oddities – bidding them fond farewell only to make space for the next project.

Shape and spirit Upholstery is all about shape and appearance on the one hand, and comfort, on the other. The good technician, one assumes will deal competently with the practicalities of lumbar rolls, stitched edges, correct gauge springs, durability, and so on. But these are merely the devices, the means; the end is the form they produce. The fundamental concept to be understood – the excellence to be pursued – is the creation of a three-dimensional shape that not only will be compatible with the frame but will also enhance it;

The frames of these two chairs are identical, but my choice of upholstery shape, top cover fabric, and decorative detail demonstrates the effect of different treatments.

The smooth, simple lines of the plain green chair are accentuated by its cover of light-catching fabric, whereas the tufted, befrilled, gathered, corded, and plumply cushioned version is full and fat, covered in chintz.

additionally and importantly, it will be functional. Regard the techniques as the "tools" to be mastered and employed to achieve your goal. Exciting upholstery is achieved not by obediently following accepted rules but by working by eye and by informed instinct, responding creatively to the frame as you build your upholstery shape.

As you progress in the subject you will appreciate that various solutions are possible – there is no absolutely correct shape for all wing chairs, all chesterfields, all tufting: uniformity is anonymous and best left to contract manufacture. The attraction of the frame lies in its individuality, and the excitement of the project derives from the choices and decisions you make in interpreting and expressing that individuality. The spirit of a chair, captured and translated with flair and confidence, will be clear to observer and sitter alike.

Shape and line The lines of upholstered shapes changed as techniques evolved, until upholstery reached its zenith in the mid- to late-19th century, when the complexity of both technique and form became gloriously one. The shapes of individual chairs, too, have often altered when they have been re-upholstered; in some cases they have been deliberately remodeled to suit changing fashions. A traditional upholsterer will tend to work a standard 19th-century-style seat on a much earlier chair and quite unknowingly create an inappropriate shape. Fortunately, research is revealing more about what the authentic shape, and thus the style, should be.

I find it remarkable that when discussing a period chair people will take into account every detail of frame construction and decoration whereas upholstery, if mentioned at all, is usually taken to mean the covering rather than the upholstery pad beneath, though this contributes as much as the frame to creating the style and lines of the chair. If this line is altered the chair will not look as the designer intended and will lose its identity. On pages 56 to 63 I consider fabrics in more detail, but here I must emphasize that there is little point in choosing sympathetic (if not authentic) fabrics for the top cover and selecting trimmings in keeping with the period style of the chair if its lines have been ignored. Even if you decide that slipcovers are more appropriate for your project you still need to understand the chair and establish its spirit, shape, and line, possibly even more so than with a permanent top cover because these attributes need to "shine through" the less body-hugging cover. For me this is a sensitive area, and my preference is for permanently fixing the shape-revealing top cover to the upholstery frame, but of course this is not always appropriate, in terms of both style and practicality. I demonstrate in two projects (pages 166 to 181) how slipcovers can be used, giving all the technical information required to achieve them.

Discovering style The early stages in re-upholstery are reminiscent of archaeology: you remove layers and sift the evidence. The process is described in detail, together with methods of keeping records, on page 65. Careful attention as you remove upholstery may simply confirm the appropriateness of the chair's treatment, but it may also

This 18th century gilt chair, known as the "Cosway chair," is thought to have been used by the English portrait painter Richard Cosway for his sitters. The shape of the original upholstery of a chair such as this would have been softly rounded to complement the curvilinear frame. Photographs of two restorations the chair has undergone this century provide a useful example of the need for an understanding of appropriate shape and technique.

This mid-20th-century restoration shows how inaccurate modern "traditional" upholsterers can be in their interpretation. The pads are meanly flat and sharply stitched, and the decoration is restricted to a simple gimp finish.

reveal interesting options and information for use on this or future projects. Hands-on investigation is both fascinating and rewarding. Even on simple frames I always feel a flutter of anticipation as the existing cover is removed. We have revealed original top covers that provide insight into a chair's age or origins. Utility covers are often clamped forbiddingly over 19th-century tufted and corded sensuousness. There are staid 18th-century frames revamped beyond recognition by the Victorians, with jigsawed curves glued and screwed to those elegant straight lines; their grotesque overstuffing proves that glorious curves and swells on one frame can become vulgar distortion on another. Frames thought to be 19th-century copies happily prove to be a century older and more valuable – or, unfortunately, vice versa.

Whether faithful restoration of a prized piece or a more casual re-creation of a more ordinary number is your aim, it is worthwhile building up awareness of what goes into the making of a seat. Study as many historical examples as possible, and "read" their overall shape. (Of course, even in the best circles an old chair may have been

In this more recent restoration of the "Cosway chair," undertaken in 1973, the crimson damask cover, decorative tufting detail and brass nail finish are sympathetic to the period of the frame. The shape of the arm pads is an improvement on the earlier restoration, but the seat would benefit from a softly rolled edge.

restored inappropriately.) As you get your eye in, you'll be surprised at the number of sofas and chairs you notice in historic buildings as well as museums, how many examples there are in paintings and prints, and the variety of styles to be "spotted" in portraits and family groups. "The Search for Style," in the following pages, gives an outline of the evolution of seat upholstery shapes and describes some of the methods used by the craftsmen of each period: a selective history, illustrated with a few of my favorite images of sofas and chairs with the people who used them. These images will help you to discover a distinctive style for your own project.

THE SEARCH
FOR STYLE

An informed approach is vital to the appropriate restoration of period chairs and sofas. It is important to learn what lies beneath the surface, to study the line the original maker intended, and to use methods that reproduce the effect. This personal journey through the evolution of upholstery techniques and styles is a selective overview which emphasizes the aspects in each century that are of particular relevance to today's upholsterers. We begin by looking at the increasing control over materials and the development of expertise in the 17th century. Form and function coincide in the 18th century and are consolidated in the great workmanship of the mid-19th. The journey ends with the turn-of-the century reaction to High Victorian opulence and with the impact of modern materials and techniques on traditional upholstery.

My purpose in this chapter is to provide some guidelines on what to look for in a period chair, so that it can be re-created in its individual spirit. Much can be learned from existing – and possibly original – upholstery and coverings. When upholstering an entire set of chairs, you may be lucky to find one that has retained its original stuffing pads. Its profile will look different from the others, and it will provide you with the information you need to re-upholster the whole set accurately.

Furniture is as useful an indicator of style and fashion as the setting in which it was placed and the clothes worn by those who used it. The images that accompany this historical survey provide further clues to finding that elusive quality, the "spirit" of the chair.

Previous pages Jean François de Troy's Reading from Molière *(detail), c. 1728, is thought to depict a fashionable Parisian banker's drawing room. It shows the generous line of 18th-century French upholstery, here on fully stuffed chairs with fat, domed nailing and rich coverings contrasting with the simple fabrics on the backs.*

The 17th Century

The centuries of Renaissance, Reformation, and expansion of Europe, when far-reaching developments were taking place on the world stage, also saw conspicuous advances in the realm of domestic comfort, including the earliest examples of what we would call upholstery. By the beginning of the 17th century it had become common practice to attach fabric and padding to a chair frame with nails. During the hundred years that followed, upholsterers broke new ground as they developed their skills in pursuit of greater control of their materials, learning to mold and to secure the stuffing and so shape the surfaces of various types of seating.

First Fixed Upholstery

The early seats with fixed upholstery – whether in X-framed or back-stool style – ranged from simple to sumptuous in the quality of materials and decoration, depending on the wealth and tastes of the owners. The exposed wooden members might be carved or turned and painted or gilded, but the basic frame was sturdy and four-square in outline, and the rudimentary upholstery consisted essentially of padding piled on the webbing or sackcloth and secured by the nailed-down fabric covering. No one had yet developed a

A simple carved X-frame chair in The Christening Feast *(detail), 1664, by Jan Steen. The rails are unwrapped, but brass nailing and a fringe are used as detailing.*

17th-century chairs achieved grandeur through sumptuously decorated top coverings. This painting, by an unknown artist, of The Somerset House Conference *(detail), 1604, which marked the end of twenty years of war between England and Spain, shows an array of X-frame chairs, typically simple in upholstery shape and technique. Several are covered from top to toe in rich fabric and trimmings. The carpet displayed on the table, as was usual at this time, contributes to the opulence of the setting in both this painting and in the one opposite.*

means of shaping the filling, but immense skill and effort went into deploying surface decoration over this primitive upholstery; the greater the owner's wealth and desire for prestige, the more sumptuous the textiles chosen and the more extravagant the embellishment and trimmings.

X-frame chairs The simple folding stools of the Middle Ages consisted of a canvas, webbing, or leather seat slung across an X-shaped frame, some with a back of similar material. The design had become highly stylized and ornamental during the 16th century and with full embellishment continued to inspire some of the most magnificent 17th-century "chairs of estate," and even royal thrones. The seat was often just webbing covered with fabric and furnished with a deep cushion, but a simple padded base might also be tacked to the frame. Comfort was insured by substantial seat and back cushions, and supreme rank declared in the extravagant wealth of the top cover and the prodigal use of fringe, tassels, and decorative nails. A dazzling mass of rich texture and color might encrust every inch of a chair, declaring opulence from the tips of its finials to its delicous fringed ankles, coyly revealing studded toenails.

These fabulous chairs lay little claim to elegance, but their vast confidence reminds me of their Victorian successors. Though more

humble in their origins, they share the same essential spirit – every surface a vehicle for proclaiming wealth and power.

Back-stools For the greater part of the 17th century the back-stool (often today called "farthingale" chairs) was the most characteristic upholstered seat. It was square-framed and generally armless, and had a gap between the rectangular backrest and the padded seat. Simple in its design and crude in its padding, it nevertheless often achieved prestige in the covering and trimming. There were certain variations in design: larger armchair versions known as "great chairs" – often covered with richer fabrics and particularly lavishly trimmed – served as seats of honor, and wider versions that could accommodate two people were occasionally made.

Upholstering the seat of a back-stool was a simple matter. Webbing was tacked to the frame (although I have seen several grand chairs of this period that appear to have had none at all). The base fabric – at this time linen sackcloth – was stretched over the webbing. Stuffing of grass, straw, tow, horsehair, or deer hair was piled on top, then the linen lining was pulled over this mound and tacked to the frame. It has been thought that the resulting domed seat, which sloped to round edges above the rail, simply reflected the fact that methods of stuffing and stitching to shape the edge filling

On the Continent, hide-covered chairs were sometimes quilted, and in this Flemish painting, Cognoscenti in a Room Hung with Pictures *(detail), c. 1620, by an unknown artist, they are also decorated with brass nails. The stitching passes through the entire upholstery pad, creating firm patterns.*

Samuel van Hoogstraten's View down the Corridor (detail), 1662, shows a sequence of rooms in which the chairs are lined up along the walls. A set of simple back-stools is covered in colorful panels of turkeywork trimmed with fringe; the chair in the room at the end has a loose cushion for comfort.

and prevent it from moving had not yet evolved. However, my more recent research indicates that this shape was quite deliberate, possibly to give the impression of a well-cushioned seat. (I feel sure, though I have no proof, that the stuffing pad in many cases might simply have been a cushion, over which the top cover was fixed to the frame.) Backs were not webbed, and inside backs tended to be completely flat in English-made chairs, since there was no means of preventing the stuffing from slipping downward. Quilting patterns stitched through top cover, stuffing, and sackcloth have, however, been recorded on chairs made in Italy, France, and Spain at this time.

Top covering Chairs were covered with plain or decorated hide – the greater the owner's wealth, the richer any painting, gilding, or embossing. Gilt leather was popular in northern and central Europe; high-quality imported Russian leather was first choice in Europe and America and had many imitations. Hide could be applied directly over the stuffing without a linen lining.

Textiles for the top cover included woolen worsted, turkeywork (a sturdy knotted fabric resembling carpet), needlework, satin or silk brocades, and silk velvets (particularly fine ones were made in Italy). Fabrics hand woven on narrow looms – only 52cm/21in wide – had to be joined on wider seats and backs. The resulting seams were frequently disguised with trimming and became a decorative feature. Late in the century bold rectangular panels outlined by mitered borders characterized Parisian seats and backs. Turkeywork was

In St. Catherine *(detail), c. 1650, by the Florentine painter Onorio Marinari, the silver and red figuring on the chairback is accentuated by gilt braid and fringe decoration. By the early 17th century, Italian upholsterers were often using damask or embossed leather. The pillow book rest is decorated with braid and tassels.*

Upholstery was a way of unifying interior decoration schemes. Self-portrait (detail), c. 1690, by Captain Thomas Smith, *shows the American artist, sitting on a chair made magnificent by massive nails, contemplating the evils of war. The red curtain, chairback, and table covering echo each other, as do the gold curtain tassel and trimming on the chair.*

woven in panels especially intended for chairs, and frames were often locally made, since the unmounted textiles were more easily transported. Frames might also be made to a particular size to accommodate a turkeywork panel in an odd width.

Decorative nails of many sizes featured prominently. Some, known as "great chair nayles," were huge and patterned with "embostynge." Nails were often arranged in patterns: leather-covered chairs were sometimes described as "double nail'd," with two parallel rows of brass nails.

The rows of brass-headed nails anchoring the plain leather gave even the simplest of chairs a measure of ornamentation. In Puritan communities, where lives (and chairs) were for service, extravagance in textiles and trimmings was proscribed, like all displays of wealth and opulence. Yet heavy brass nailing was used to fix the leather to the frame of the back-stool that came to be known as the "Cromwellian" chair. The fact that these nails appeared functional apparently excused their decorative appearance. Dull iron tacks would, of course, have served to fix the hide – so perhaps these gleaming domes represent a minor triumph of gaiety over sobriety.

These leather-covered back-stools have a quiet dignity. Their more ornamental fabric-covered and be-tasseled cousins, a few of which survive in historical institutions and stately homes, flaunt the remnants of their fabulous garments over their wide, flat backs and bony unpadded arms – once magnificent and now endearingly gauche. In view of the simplicity of this early upholstery, it is quite wrong to craft a double-stuffed stitched "traditional" square-edged seat on a 17th-century frame; and reproduction chairs certainly gain character with a minimum of sophistication in their underpinnings.

Control of Comfort

Upholstery techniques as we now know them made special progress toward the end of the 17th century. Lack of technical expertise, concealed beneath sophisticated trimmings and fabrics, was succeeded by a much greater control of the medium. Upholstery was able to develop a firm, fluid line as chair frames became more curvilinear. Cabriole legs and gently curving backs were perfectly complemented by the confident lines of smoothly flowing upholstery. The use of various methods of twine stitching to secure stuffing – often drawing directly on saddlery techniques – prevented sagging and gave the upholsterer better control of shape.

Tufted squabs Back-stools had their parallels in other forms of functional chairs, including the "Dutch chair," with turned members and a rush seat, and chairs with caned backs and seats produced in Holland and England in the latter half of the 17th century. These were rendered more comfortable with loose cushions rather than with fixed upholstery. When, in the early 1700s, the French adopted the caning technique (by then losing favor elsewhere) and created caned chairs to designs of their own, they equipped them with shaped squab cushions tied in place.

Squabs had been used on daybeds, sofas, and other types of seating produced in France during the last quarter of the 17th century, and this marked a new vogue for reclining instead of sitting upright – at least in bedchambers and the more informal rooms of a house. Squabs were essentially small mattresses with low box sides. The tightly packed stuffing (whether hair, wool, feathers and down, straw, or grasses) was kept evenly distributed by being stitched through at intervals, as with quilting. Tufting ties – a small bunch of unspun threads – kept the quilting thread from passing back through the covering canvas into the stuffing. Some upholsterers came to see the tuft as a decoration in its own right, and in the 18th century took to using it to make a pattern through the top cover.

In The Physician's Visit *(detail), c. 1660, by Jan Steen, the rudimentary upholstery on the back-stool is typical of the period. Here the upright rails (which were seen from the front) are wrapped, but the back rails that faced the wall are left bare.*

Squab mattresses were also sometimes used as the stuffing base for seats beneath the fixed top cover on couches. Daybeds for reclining had one fixed, inclined arm which was lightly stuffed. Improved techniques for keeping stuffing in place on the vertical surfaces of arms and backrests had also been developed. Like the ratchet adjustments that made it possible to fix these parts of the seat at appropriately comfortable angles, much of this new expertise had evolved out of the need to make chairs for invalids. It was fashion, however, with its increasing emphasis on informality, that popularized such seating.

Twine ties Curled horsehair, increasingly used in the last quarter of the century to stuff chair backs, was controlled by the use of stitching techniques. On some English chairs twine was taken across the inside backs of chairs, under the linen lining, and tacked to the side rails; it

From the mid-17th century, sets of French engravings were sold to show new forms of furniture and upholstery in fashionable settings. This mattress, on its upholstered fixed base, is enhanced by a fat be-tasseled bolster. A comparatively short fringe on the bottom rail reveals an amusingly zoomorphic clawed foot.

wove through the stuffing and helped to hold it in place. These chairs consequently developed a different profile, and the now elongated backs could be fairly fully stuffed; surviving chairs of the period have a rather pot-bellied look, conferring a portly distinction to their now venerable age. Armrests were also padded with stuffing, which was not stitched to the linen lining and so has also sagged. However, such chairs no longer share the whimsicality of earlier great chairs, with their suggestion of scrawny, malnourished arms clad in luxurious sleeves.

The edge roll By the third quarter of the 17th century upholsterers were using stuffed edge rolls for seat fronts on wing chairs (then known as "easy chairs"), creating a well into which a cushion fitted. In essence this was the platform, or deck, as we know it today. The edge roll is crucial to the evolution of upholstery shape. Craftsmen quickly appreciated that it could be used not only to help retain a cushion on a base but also to shape and support stuffing within a fixed cover, and so it was adopted for general seating.

The roll is made by stitching a border of linen to the sackcloth about 7-10cm/3-4in from the edge of the rail. This is then firmly stuffed, and the linen is tacked off along the rail. Edge rolls are attached to side and front rails, and the center of the seat pad is generously stuffed. Short bridle ties stitched through the sackcloth also retain the stuffing more successfully than the single rail-to-rail

These late 17th-century engravings illustrate chairs with similar high-backed upholstery shapes but different decorative treatments.

Left *The mitered braid on the inside back is used to divide the top cover into a series of framed reliefs. Flat braid is fastened with brass nails on the extreme edge of the inside back.*

Right *The wide braid and fringe frames the edge of the inside back and the seat pads.*

These two paintings demonstrate the contrast between the lines of 17th- and 18th-century furniture. Above *The chairs in* A French Bedchamber *(detail), c. 1690, by an unknown artist, have the slightly domed, high stuffed backs typical of fashionable styles in late 17th-century France. The red velvet covers are trimmed with gold fringe and brass nailing, but the outside backs appear to be uncovered, showing the sackcloth.* Opposite *François-Hubert Drouais's portrait is of Madame de Pompadour, Louis XV's mistress, who had a great influence on French taste. Painted in 1763, it also depicts the full, sensuous curves of both frame and upholstery shapes that developed in France in the 18th century. The rich fabric, gilt frames, and gimp finish all contribute to the sumptuous effect. The table is inlaid with Sèvres porcelain.*

loop used earlier. There were local variations: rolls of marsh grass wrapped in linen or canvas were used on some American chairs.

A method of stitching the stuffing to the linen lining to create a firm, square edge was also developing. The earliest example that I have investigated is in the original upholstery of the Duke's Bedchamber chairs at Ham House, near London, dated 1675.

Top covers Increasing control of shape was matched by exuberant top covers. Tapestries – the best of which came from the Beauvais, Aubusson, and Gobelins factories in France – were woven in panels to fit the upholstered pads of furniture. Chinoiserie designs, with figures and landscapes, and panels of *petit* and *gros point* needlework, often stitched in wool and highlighted with silk, became popular.

The 18th Century

During the 18th century, chair design was, I believe, unsurpassed. Superb line and proportion combined with upholstery expertise to provide comfortable and elegant repose, which accorded well with a new degree of attention to style of decoration in interiors generally. All the components of present-day traditional upholstery were gradually assembled – good, quality workmanship refining techniques and producing superb designs that were generous but not

extravagant. Form and function became truly united.

Few seats have survived from the 17th century, but one is more likely to be able to observe restoration of 18th-century pieces at first hand, and some readers may actually carry it out. However, many pieces have been abused by later upholsterers. On sofas, for example, the straight slope of round-topped arms into the sweeping curve of the back rail has been coarsened with thick, overstuffed "traditional" upholstery. The backs and arms of original sofas that I have examined, on the other hand, were not stitched. The tops of the arms were padded sparingly – enough for comfort, but not so much as to thicken the line. The inside arm stuffing was generous and

comfortable, but not bulbous, and the inside back was stuffed in the same manner. A similarly restrained approach is evident in easy chairs.

Seats on curved sofas were edge-rolled or straight-edged, as on armchairs (described below). I have noticed that straight frames on good late 18th-century "country" pieces – by this I mean most furniture other than that in grand houses – often have edge-roll seats, with a gently curved front edge, rather than the more fashionable straight edge. This is because it is probable that fashions (and certain that methods) took longer to become common practice in the provinces. Personally I prefer this kind of curved-edge seat to a straight edge, unless it is to be piped, tufted, and close-nail finished.

Two sets of armchairs that I have worked on demonstrate classic 18th-century upholstery techniques in the service of a particular style. The two are in fact parallel English interpretations of the French easy chair, or *fauteuil*. This classic French chair, developed in the second half of the 17th century, had open arms, a stuffed back and huge down cushions, often reaching the height of the chair arms. Its curving lines, capaciousness, and abundant stuffing were being "copied" in other countries by the mid-18th century, but its potent blend of elegance and largesse was never quite achieved. On the English translations with curved frames, the upholstery was flatter, and, as the straight line developed with square legs and frame, the upholstery accentuated this look.

Each of the twin English developments of the *fauteuil* exemplifies a distinct and characteristic "look": one style is curvilinear, while the other has straight lines and is cleanly piped and bordered. In both, the underlying structure achieves its effect with masterly simplicity.

The Curved Line

In this type of chair the upholstery flows into the curves of the frame in a typical version of what the English called the "French chair." The seat is created with the stuffed edge roll and central stuffing (already described) and has a linen lining. The curve of the firm, gently rounded edge harmonizes perfectly with the lines of the frame – though the upholstery is considerably flatter than on the *fauteuil* which was its original inspiration.

The inside back has a single web from center top to bottom and one from side to side, sackcloth, and stuffing into bridle ties. The linen lining is tacked over and the stuffing is shaped to form a curved, softly compact edge by means of a single row of twine "blind" running stitches through the linen. One row of stitches to draw the stuffing to the edge was also used on single chairs with curved back frames.

The arms are stuffed and stitched in the same fashion. It is very important to note and, if necessary, re-create the correct arm shape; often the originals are replaced with aggressively top stitched and stuffed armpads that are square and harsh. The pad should curve deliciously like a baby's arm – a chubby swell gliding into the wrist.

These chairs are commonly finished with two characteristic 18th-century decorative touches – tufting and brass nailing (p31).

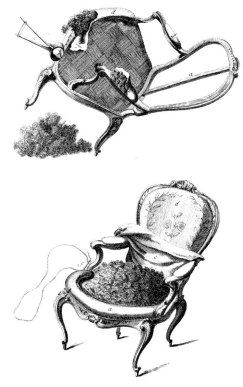

Through the Rococo period, French upholstery lines remained full.

Opposite *In* The Inconsolable Widow *(detail), c. 1763, by Jean-Baptiste Greuze, the flowing pose of the sitter is accentuated by the generosity of the classic* fauteuil. *The huge cushion stuffed with down reaches the height of the well padded chubby arms, and large nails emphasize the lines. The French* fauteuil *was imitated throughout Europe, but never satisfactorily.*

Above *These engravings from Diderot's famous* Encyclopédie, *1751–70, portray the manufacture of a French armchair. The first shows the French method of close webbing a seat; the rail construction of the back makes webbing unnecessary here. In the second seat, sackcloth is not depicted, and there is a stitched edge roll at the front rail.*

The Straight Line

Many mid-18th-century armchairs of the "Chippendale" type were based on straight lines and a four-square outline which called for a correspondingly square-profiled upholstery – usually emphasized by piping. A method I have seen on a number of contemporary seats (and accordingly have used to restore many others) involves constructing flat, firm walls to support the clean lines. For accurate re-creation of the technique, the process involves webbing the inside back with a single central web from top to bottom and from side to side, and applying sackcloth. Borders of linen are tacked down to the sides of the top and side rails. For a slight broadening below the arm joints, allowance is made for the swell of the lumbar region, and overall for seams. The back is stuffed to bridle ties with full, firm quantities at the bordered edges. Rows of blind running stitches are worked in twine through the linen and horsehair, to build a firm, straight edge. Much practice is needed to achieve firm, flat walls: the secret is to keep stitch tension uniform throughout. A linen cover or lid is tacked to the back base rail and pinned, with raw edges inward, to the borders and then joined with tiny overstitches.

This beautifully crafted and deceptively simple edge must always have been, as it is now, a very lengthy process. Soon, edge stitching methods were to be developed to make the all-in-one stitched edge (described below) which is still used today.

The arms of the straight-line chair were worked as described above for the "curved-line" type of chair. The seat was sometimes bordered and worked in the same way as the inside back, but another method was often employed, and it is this one that I use if working from scratch. The seat is webbed and covered with sackcloth as usual. Next an edge roll is worked on the sides and the front and stuffed to the required height. Linen borders are then tacked to the rails and the seat is stuffed and stitched as on the inside back. The running stitches pass through the edge roll (the first row being fastened to the frame with tacks), which gives a tremendous amount of support and strength. Along with the firmly stitched border seam, this squares the shape. This combination of edge roll and bordered stitching is stronger than the method without the edge roll, but I have seen them both in their original form.

The top cover on both back and seat is piped and bordered. Outside backs were usually covered in a plain harmonizing fabric such as wool, which was less expensive than the silks, velvets, and damasks. If true authenticity is sought when re-upholstering, the top cover fabric should be cut to the original 52cm/21in width and seamed; it is quite remarkable how much difference this apparently trivial detail will make to the finished chair.

Single chairs with square backs were upholstered in the same way as armchairs; the simpler variety, however, was not bordered and stitched on the inside back, and the gentle stuffing swell curved into the flat clean edges of the frame.

American straight-rail chairs of the period, like English armchairs, were strictly square in their upholstery, but the techniques used were different. A superb method of "over-the-rail" upholstery involved

The English 18th-century straight line looked deceptively simple, but required the beautiful crafting epitomized by these two chairs. **Above** *John Linnel's design for a chair with tufted seat and back, c. 1760, has what appears to be a piped or corded and brass nail finish.* **Opposite** *In this Portrait of Mrs. Thomas Boylston (detail) 1766, by the Bostonian painter John Singleton Copley, the arm of the chair has a simple curve, and the straight line of the upholstery pad is accentuated by piped seaming. The chair has tufting, a hand-woven lustrous damask top cover – the seam can be seen on the back – and brass nail finish. English taste was the main influence in America at this period.*

strips of webbing instead of linen borders and a different type of stitched edge roll (known as a "French roll" and tightly stitched to make a "French edge"). The linen was tightly whipstitched along the top of the webbing of the French edge, forming a crisp right angle.

The all-in-one stitched edge As the 18th century drew to a close, upholsterers were developing the final stages of "traditional" upholstery methods as they are taught today. The bordered and stitched edge roll for square shapes, requiring time-consuming stitching, was eliminated by a method very similar to that practiced

now. In this new method a single piece of linen – later to be replaced by scrim – is positioned over the stuffing and tacked to the rails. The edge stitches along the front and side rails pass through the front of the linen, through the stuffing, out through the top of the linen and back down to the front again, forming a looped stitch on the top of the linen (which will be the top of the seat pad). The earlier running stitch has become a backstitch, which is stronger, and which later progresses to become the locked blind stitch we use today (p89). Each successive row of stitching compresses the side and top linen and brings its stuffing content nearer to the top of the wall. A well is formed on the top of the seat, which is top-stuffed into bridle ties as it is today, with a linen lining overall. The difference between this and today's method is the fact that we work blind stitches that do not pass through the top of the scrim for the first row or rows, according to the height and shape of the edge we are building.

Decorative Finishes

Tufting, brass nailing, braid, and tape had become popular in England by 1750 but took another 20 years or so to become fashionable in France. Recent evidence suggests that in America tufting (where the term today denotes buttoning) was being used in the latter part of the century.

Tufting Developed as a method of regulating and retaining the stuffing in mattresses and squabs, tufting was initially concealed beneath a top cover. Used to serve the same purpose on fixed upholstery, it became a decorative feature that is still used today (p110). Tufts were short strands of silk or linen threads, tied in the center and looped through the top cover and the stuffing on long twines. They were then tied off beneath the sackcloth at the back of the chairback and arms and underneath the seat, compressing the upholstery where they were pulled tight. The tufts themselves resemble little brush heads. The twine is tied off to a comfortable tension, forming restrained indentations; too tightly fastened, it tends to make cross-tensions that flatten the upholstery and disturb the eye, and also to distort the lines of the seams. The positioning of the tufting should be sympathetic to the shape of the chair. Curved chairs usually have a curved top row of tufts on the inside back. The middle, straight row is usually a little above the arm-joints: if level with the arms, the chair is visually widened and its proportions distorted.

Where an old chair retains its original sackcloth, any tufting patterns can be seen from the tie holes – even if the remnants of the ties themselves have disappeared. New tufting can then be carried out according to the original design.

Brass nailing Generally larger than those in use today, brass nails were higher-domed and had square shanks. They were positioned close together, with just a tiny breathing space. Patterns varied and could be quite complicated, with double rows and curves. In very grand rooms, both the top cover and nailing patterns on the

Flat, straight, clean lines were achieved by slender padding during the 18th century.
Opposite *The restrained upholstery of the sofa depicted in front of a late 18th-century tapestry design, after Boucher, with its straight edges and simple padding, relies on the top cover and elaborate gilded frame for a sense of exuberance.*
Below *A turn-of-the-century design for a parlor chair, from Thomas Sheraton's Encyclopædia, published in 1805. It has a tufted squab and knotted top cover with interesting detail at the corners; the pin-stuffed back is finished with gimp.*

*The contrasting styles of the mid-
and late-18th century are clearly
shown in these two famous French
paintings.*
Above *François Boucher's
Reclining Girl (detail), 1752,
captures the luscious comfort of
this deep mattress on its rounded
platform base. The baggy pillow
further emphasizes the sensuality
and provocative pose of the figure.*
Opposite *Jean-Louis David's
portrait of Madame Récamier,
1800, helped to spread the fashion
for day beds with flowing Grecian
lines. The slender padding on the
side scrolls contrasts with the softer
comfort of the mattress and
bolsters, both of which are trimmed
to accentuate the blue fabric. The
Récamiers' house, redecorated in
the neo-classical style, caused a
sensation in Republican Paris.*

furniture would often complement those on the walls.

Careful study of original chair rails will enable the restorer to
follow the original nailing pattern. The chair may well have been
close-nailed more than once, so look for a series of wider-spaced
square holes, usually sited slightly higher up the rail to accommodate
the larger-diameter head. Rails may, of course, need repair before
they can be nailed again in the same pattern.

The 19th Century

Vast quantities of upholstered furniture survive from the 19th
century, reflecting the sheer amount produced – and mass-produced,
as the Industrial Revolution took effect. Technological advances and
rising living standards made comfortable seating more widely
available, not only to the increasingly prosperous middle classes, but
also to a new working-class market. Reflecting the breadth and
complexity of this social setting is an enormous variety of
upholstered forms.

The relatively sober mood in which the century begins and ends
tends to be eclipsed by the notorious High Victorian exuberance,
reminiscent of the 17th-century love of splendor and display

(though achieved with considerably greater expertise). A riot of shapes, patterns, and textures expresses the High Victorian bourgeois, master of his world, secure in his power and prestige, smug in his prosperity and material possessions. The peculiar moral duality of the times is evident in the cord-lashed rolls, the button-fastened swells and lavish curves – sensuality both visual and tactile, yet in the respectable context of furniture.

At the same time cheap upholstered chairs were made for the masses from poor-quality materials and packed with inferior stuffings, such as wool and cotton refuse, wood shavings, and moss. Frames were often made from unseasoned timber; I have often found tack rails with the bark still on them, or made from packing crates. However poor the quality, the fact is that these chairs do still totter into upholstery workshops a hundred years later. Stuffings such as wood shavings have certainly proved durable, but are very unpleasant to rip out and must have created dreadful working conditions for the original upholsterers.

Formal Angularity

The first three decades of the century – the period summed up as "Regency" in England, "Empire" in France, and "Federal" in the United States – saw some truly uncomfortable upholstery. For some time the seated comfort of the fashionable was sacrificed to the supremely

disciplined lines of stylized furniture nostalgic for ancient Greece and Egypt.

The squareness that had been developing in upholstered forms during the 18th century became aggressively angular. The all-in-one stitched edge previously described was honed to a blade-like fineness. A row of small knotted blanket stitches at the extreme top edge of the stitched walls gave an absolutely defined line. When well crafted, this edge is virtually indestructible and gives superb definition. Sharp defined edges were allied to firm, flat surfaces, often shaped to the curve of the frame. First stuffing pads were firmly lashed down with stuffing ties. Top stuffing, while adequate, was not allowed to interfere with the line. Springs were not yet in general use, and the resulting seats and backs were hard and unyielding.

Even when cushions were part of the design, their purpose seems often to have owed more to visual balance than to comfort. Stitched horsehair squabs and cushions were a feature on couches, ottomans, and sofas. The vogue for angularity actually manifested itself in *square* bolsters. Softer cushions were sometimes draped over the hard bolsters and base squabs, with decorative corners, cord-tied, pleated, or sometimes giving the appearance of slipcovers bow-tied over fixed covers.

The first half of the 19th century saw a move from severe Regency angularity to the more informal early Victorian style.

Opposite *This magazine plate shows the solidity of the bench-stool – the child has not even dented the upholstery pad. Its square lines are in marked contrast to the delicacy of the elaborate trellis fringe.*

Below *Charlotte Bosanquet's* The Drawing Room at Vintners, Kent *(detail), c. 1840, is furnished with chairs and sofas with pretty but utilitarian slipcovers. Removed for special occasions, such coverings were widely used in the 19th century. The pole screen to the right of the hearth protected the women's faces from the heat of the fire.*

Outlines might be further defined by decorative cords instead of cording, and bolsters, cushions and squabs were often tasseled. Fringe was again fashionable, but applied in a delicate trellis pattern.

The Softer Line

As the 19th century advanced and the Victorian era began, changing fashions led to a desire for informality, a more relaxed and comfortable style than the self-conscious angularity of the Regency. One major advance in upholstery technique that brought a whole new dimension to comfort and design in seating was the introduction of reliable springing. The use of springs became increasingly widespread during the 1830s, with this gradual shift in emphasis toward comfort.

Springing Sprung seats of various kinds are recorded as far back as the late 18th century, but their use was limited until improvements in the quality of steel and advances in manufacturing techniques made it possible to produce suitably resilient models in quantity. It was only toward the middle of the 19th century that upholsterers perfected techniques for efficiently tying in springs, very much as we do today (p93), and for preventing the springs from moving around independently in a seat, with the attendant risk of chafing and snapping the inadequate twine ties and making the seat lumpy. While on the one hand custom upholsterers were incorporating

Buttoning, a purely stylistic device, became very popular in the 19th century.
Below *Mary Ellen Best's watercolor of her drawing room in Worms, 1846/7, shows a sofa and chair with the informal, soft deep buttoning of the early Victorian period.*
Opposite *Three designs from a German journal on interior decoration, 1871, showing different pleated tufting effects.*

springs into their best-quality hand-crafted pieces, at the other end of the market sprung seats formed one stage in a production line that put moderately priced, reasonably comfortable seating within reach of huge new sectors of the population. By the late 19th century framed sets of springs were being factory made in "units" with steel wire defining the shape of the seat.

The ingenious use of springs allowed the skilled and imaginative upholsterer full rein and enabled him to create an extraordinary range of convoluted shapes on a single frame. Seats, arms, and inside backs were sprung, and very soon double springing was combined with clever use of sizes and gauges to produce some amazing creations. Such springing added considerably to the comfort of a chair, however tightly packed the stuffing in the buttons and channels.

Buttoning and tufting As the tailored line of upholstery became softer, tufting became fashionable again as a method of securing stuffing. From the late 1830s "rosettes" of twisted thread or covered buttons replaced the tufts, a method that has now become known as "deep" buttoning (though, paradoxically, it is shallow compared to pleated tufting). Small buttons were tied off through a cover cut larger than its base, with thicker stuffing below creating a soft, cushiony look. Many surviving photographs of this period clearly show deep buttoning. Its casual air, with a puckered and almost baggy-looking top cover, is a definite style, and should be re-created if the frame of your chair dates from this time. Unfortunately, many upholsterers today scathingly dismiss this as a shoddy example of pleated tufting, and re-upholster using the latter, misguidedly correcting what they take to be the poor workmanship of the original upholsterer and, in so doing, destroying the authenticity and charm of the style's comfortable informality. Rules that have been learned unquestioningly in training can be difficult to disregard and are all too often put routinely and inappropriately into practice. Buttoning provides one with a good opportunity of first studying the shape and overall look to be achieved, and then using the appropriate upholstery techniques that will achieve it.

Curved Opulence

The mid-Victorians considered that the ornamentation of any surface, in any material – wood, metal, ceramics, etc. – enhanced its opulence and thus bestowed prestige on the owner. Upholstery was no exception. No longer merely an equal partner with its frame, it soon dominated – and in many cases consumed – the frame, enveloping every vestige of the structure. Seat, arm, and back edges were not simply straight or curved, but had pillow edges, bible edges, scrolled, rolled and gathered edges – and in many instances, edges that disappeared entirely.

Pleated tufting By the late 1840s a system of deep first and second stuffing, into which buttons could be fastened, had been developed. It is commonly thought that pleated tufting evolved as a functional

necessity to hold the very thick stuffing in place, but it was quite the reverse: a technique was devised for purely stylistic ends. Stuffing is held very firmly within its bridle, stuffing, and stitching ties, and requires nothing more to keep it in place. Indeed, the first stuffing pad has to be cut to create the depth required for true pleated tufting.

The area of the top cover was necessarily greater, in a carefully calculated ratio, than that of the sackcloth, or burlap, to which it was held. The excess fabric was dispersed into regular diagonal folds, and the edges were "tacked off clean" – smooth and unpuckered, with pleats of material running vertically and horizontally from the button to the edge rails.

In the 1860s and '70s pleated tufting became immensely popular and reached extremes of sophistication and skill on the part of the upholsterer. Although we speak in terms of comfort in describing 19th-century seat furniture, much of it would have been very firm. Padding was indeed deep, but was stuffed firmly and buttressed quite rigidly within its corset of buttons, rolls, and cords. Like a good saddle, a firmly buttoned chair would have to be worn in. In order to re-create this style one must really appreciate the spirit of the time. Restrained pleated tufting, with a flat "fried-egg" look, may constitute technical accuracy, but the chair will not boast or sing, or even hum; it will be consigned to ill-befitting anonymity. Many periods have a characteristic curving line, but the Victorian curve was a great swell – no restrained understatement here, but an indulgence in opulence and sensuality. Be aware that you are re-creating curves and valleys into which the cords and buttons will nestle invitingly: they are not merely devices to fix the top cover and disguise seams.

Iron framing As upholstery became more diverse in shape and style, so did the chair frames themselves. Seating for every imaginable purpose and of every shape and size was created. Simple formal elegance was gone: chairs littered rooms like bric-à-brac, many of

Conversation seats were one of the most popular of the new shapes, often achieved through iron-frame construction.

Opposite *A design for an exuberant conversation seat, from a German journal of 1871. Deep buttoned throughout and copiously decorated with cords, tassels, and fringes, it is crowned with an equally elaborate four-cornered vase.*

Below *In* Conversation Piece *(detail), 1884, by Solomon J. Solomon, a courting couple share the intimacy of a conversation seat during an evening of musical entertainment in a cluttered Victorian parlor.*

Late 19th-century upholstery reflected either the elaborate effects of High Victorianism or the simpler styles born of a reaction against excess. In Girl in a Blue Armchair, *1878, by the American painter Mary Cassatt, the gentle comfort of these chairs, possibly constructed on iron frames, is evident from the relaxed pose of the young girl.*

them unsuited to any purpose. Ottomans became incredible confections like giant wedding cakes, ascending tiers of valances, rolls, buttons, and channels, topped with cascading flowers and plants. There were conversation seats, love seats, prayer chairs, boudoir chairs – some in ridiculously frivolous shapes made possible by advances in metal technology. Iron frames (sometimes termed wire frames) bent into exaggerated curves were bolted to the timber seat frames, creating many shapes that would have been either impracticable or impossible to produce in timber. The more sensible and restrained of these chairs, with their well-fitting lumbar rolls and gently yielding wire backs, accommodate the sitter very happily. Because these metal frames are indestructible, many are still in use today (p138).

Chairs and sofas were often bolted together end to end, back to back, in circular and serpentine shapes. Many of these have since been separated but still bear the metal fixtures, which must be disguised in some way.

Top covers The over-the-top effects of texturing were further exaggerated by the use of rich, heavily patterned and colored top fabrics. Many of these fabrics remain on the chair frames, usually faded and worn, but when the time comes for repair and replacement and their century-old creases are released at tack-off points and around buttons, the original brilliant colors are clearly visible. Garish aniline dyes also colored the needlepoint designs worked in tent or cross stitch and known as Berlin wool work; these were often used to cover upholstery. The same colors were found in the carpet panels woven to fit upholstered furniture for popular consumption. Again, tucked-away sections have to be seen so that their vivid colors can be appreciated.

More sober was haircloth, woven from horsehair and usually in black. It was extremely serviceable and, in my opinion, very smart, but it could never, I fear, have been very comfortable. Those black horsehair-covered sofas in the front parlor hardly sound inviting.

The Changing Line

With the confidence of the High Victorians, upholstery forms had swept up in a crescendo of stuffing and springing, enveloped in a profusion of buttons, corded rolls, scrolls, fringes, tassels, and valances. Buttoning mania was receding by the 1880s, although it remained popular, but upholstery retained its ornate opulence. Now smooth non-buttoned areas on backs and seats were bordered and shaped by stuffed rolls and channels – themselves lusciously gathered, buttoned, and corded. The busy effect was often exaggerated by using contrasting fabrics: outside backs and arms, borders, corded rolls, and valances might be in plain velvet, while harmonizing brocade or damask covered internal surfaces. Almost every conceivable finishing decoration was used – wherever possible, it seems, all on the same chair. As in the estate chairs of the 17th century, swaying tassel-layered fringes, cords and ropes, gimps and rosetted tassels provided the sumptuous finale to the already extravagant production.

Not everyone, however, subscribed to such lavish ornamentation. By the last quarter of the 19th century, the very excesses of the period had inspired a number of reactions in the direction of cleaner

Plate for a sofa design by Carl Hettwig, 1833. A sumptuous effect is created by the use of corded rolls in contrasting fabric, which demanded highly skilled upholstery work, three different fabrics, tassels, and tasseled fringes.

The turn of the century saw a return to simpler lines. The sofa in Arachne, 1893, by Carlo Stratta, has gently curved stuffing without tufting and is covered in a light pastel fabric. The Japanese influence is evident in the delicate wallpaper.

lines and simpler styles. A new form of Victorian eclecticism incorporated ideas from the Aesthetic Movement, influenced by Japanese designs. A nostalgia for the 18th century was manifested in "Queen Anne," "after-Chippendale," and various other vaguely classical styles. The English Arts and Crafts Movement (paralleled in America by the Mission Style) was making its impact. The simpler designs of Morris & Co. appealed initially only to connoisseurs of hand-crafted items, but eventually grew to have great influence on manufactured design. The stylized rectilinear show-wood frames of designers such as Godwin, Voysey, and Mackintosh allowed for only the cleanest and simplest of upholstery lines achieved by sculpting the stuffing into gentle curves, or by discreet springing – neither involving any innovation or refinement of upholsterers' techniques. French Art Nouveau designers such as Gallé and Majorelle were creating writhing plant-like structures with sinuously carved frames and sympathetic upholstery which flowed into the fluid outlines.

In mass manufacture, too, lighter frames supported sleeker upholstery. On many slender frames with narrow tapering legs, the gross overstuffing of the previous era gave way to the virtually anorexic, and seats were merely pin-stuffed (p78). Sturdier furniture was sensibly upholstered in proportion to the frame, as the excesses of the 19th century waned. And as heavy, rich fabrics, swagged draperies, fringe, tassels, and clutter abated, the lighter colors and fabrics were more simply finished with brass nails or gimp.

The 20th Century

By the turn of the century the High Victorian frenzy of ornamentation had subsided in favor of simpler surfaces and straighter lines. Until after the first World War, "traditional" upholstery materials and methods continued unaltered. In the 1920s and '30s the average British home possessed its "three-piece suite" – a pair of armchairs and a small sofa – which fitted into the front parlors of modest houses. Larger homes boasted similar styles on a more generous

In Wyndham Lewis's portrait of Dame Edith Sitwell, 1923–35, the setting emphasizes the subject's angular features and clothes. The square back and curved seat of the chair show how upholstery was used to create shapes adapted to cleaner lines.

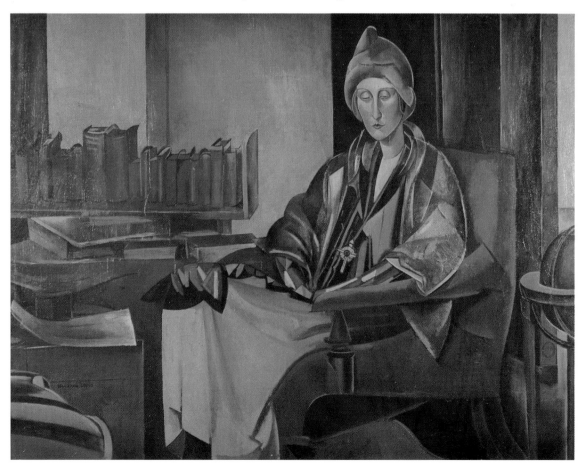

scale. The overstuffed modern furniture of the 1920s had springs and wire edges: stuffed and stitched traditionally, the smooth full padding, roundly comfortable, was covered in a variety of fabrics, especially hides or leather cloth, velour or mohair, tapestry, cut moquette, damask, or printed cotton.

Designers continued to employ the upholstered shape as an integral part of the overall design for the mainstream market, but new materials such as steel, laminates, and plastics were stimulating experiment and change. Frames with timber rails for tacking traditional upholstery were no longer the rule. Indeed, hide- and canvas-slung tubular steel (in styles somewhat reminiscent of the 17th-century X-framed stools), and molded laminate and plastic frames required no padding at all.

The arrival of foam padding revolutionized the upholstery trade. No longer were years of training needed to acquire skills, or days of labor to execute these skills on a single frame. Pads could be made in a moment with glue and staple-guns and could be sculpted into all sorts of new shapes. Inevitably the "traditional" upholsterer became an endangered species, working mainly in the restoration of antiques.

Foam has retained its supremacy, but perhaps change is again afoot. As the hazards of toxic fumes from burning foam have become more widely recognized, a demand for traditional fillings has re-emerged. This does not – and cannot – mean a return to hand-stuffing and stitching in true traditional style; the labor costs would be prohibitive. Prevailing conditions are thus subjecting

In the 20th century, technological innovation has contributed to the changing line. "Modern Bedroom in Vivid Coloring," from a book on upholstery published in 1937, illustrates the simplicity of modernist upholstery shapes, often achieved by the use of foam and spring units.

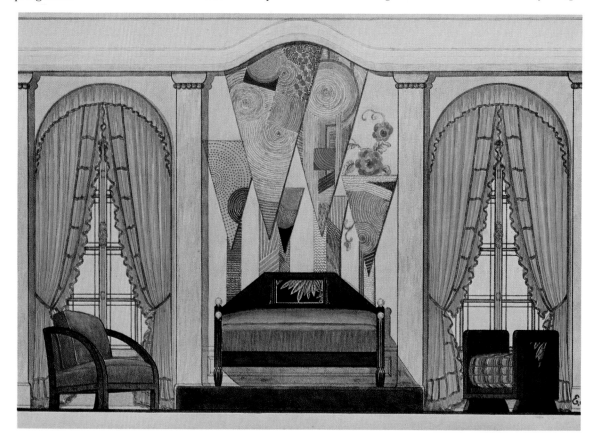

upholstery to yet another swing, with popular design being influenced by public demand and labor costs. Many modern sofas and armchairs now have feather cushions for seats and backs, replacing the need for labour-intensive fixed, stuffed and stitched pads. Together with spring unit seats, knock-down assembly work, powered staple-guns, and so on, this keeps the cost of comfortable upholstery using traditional materials within the price range of most households – as has been the case for the past century.

But with all the brilliant technology utilized by today's most efficient and reputable manufacturers, I find it comforting to know that ultimately the materials still need to be fixed to the frame by human hands.

The late 20th century has seen a move back toward traditional shapes. In Dennis Rolland at Home in New York, 1986, Gillian Barlow has placed the subject in a room as cluttered with furnishings and ornaments as a Victorian parlor.

EQUIPMENT, MATERIALS & TECHNIQUES

Equipment & Materials

The basic tools and materials of this traditional craft have been passed down to us from our 18th-century predecessors with very little change. They are simple, effective, and inexpensive – an ideal combination to encourage the beginner. I feel sure that my choice of career must have been significantly influenced by the fact that the tools were within my reach, both financially and physically.

If your aim is to attain skill in the craft, I strongly recommend that you equip yourself with a good set of professional tools. They are precisely designed in terms of size and balance to enable you to develop a rhythm of working that will aid your dexterity. Household substitutes can be found, but the results will not bear comparison (a magnetic upholsterer's hammer, for instance, has nothing to do with an all-purpose tool of the same name). In time your tools will become old friends and, with practice, an extension of your hands.

It is notoriously difficult to acquire the tools and materials of the trade. Large department stores, professional upholsterers and teachers, or a mail order specialist are some sources that I would suggest. Be guided by the list on the following pages, which recommends the equipment that I find particularly useful, but be prepared to accept that your choice may be limited.

The larger workshop equipment is also relatively simple, but here I feel that there is room for "making do" with improvisation until you have decided on your own requirements and can afford and accommodate professional equipment.

The Workspace

A specially built workspace is truly a luxury. In reality you will probably be working in any available space, from a spare bedroom to a garage. You will have to make the most of what you have, but comfortable working conditions will contribute to your ease of working and, ultimately, to successful results.

Light and space are primary considerations. You will need good light both above and all around your work. If light sources are limited, have a lamp with a flexible arm that you can re-position as necessary. You must have enough space to allow you to move freely, and to move the work without damage.

Access to the workspace must also be considered: can you move your project in and out without hazards, particularly when it is finished with expensive new top cover and is possibly several centimeters/inches larger with new padding?

Organize your tools and materials so that they are readily accessible. The toolbox should be comfortably at hand – I usually keep mine on an old dining chair that can be moved around. Set aside an area for your materials and keep them as neat as possible. It is much easier to work when you can lay your hands on threads and scissors without being exasperated by their elusiveness. It is also a great benefit to have the sewing machine threaded and ready for use.

General Equipment

Trestles A certain amount of work can be done on a table top, but you will soon discover that a good pair of trestles (also called horses) is invaluable. Trestles are commercially available, but it is better to have them custom-built.

They must support the work at a height that is comfortable for you. The top should have a lip all around to provide a channel to take the legs of chairs and sofas. The main supporting stretcher should be centrally positioned so that the trestles can be brought closer together when working on a chair sitting on its seat rails with the legs hanging down astride the trestles.

The photograph shows the design of the trestles I use, the only type that I can work with. I use one pair at a height of 80cm/31in for most work and a pair half that height when working on upright backs.

Leather padding on the lip will protect your work from being damaged by the wood.

Cutting table I use a large sheet of thick (12mm/½in) particle board with two strips of softwood screwed to the underside; this sits on the top of the trestles, stabilized by the battening. This "table" provides me with a large surface for cutting out top cover, making cushions, and much other work. I store it upright against a wall when not in use.

Sewing machine I use a heavy-duty industrial machine, but your own domestic model should suffice if you use large needles for heavier materials. If you need to stitch leather (especially if it is to be piped) cut and mark your work and ask a professional upholsterer or drapery maker to stitch it for you.

Button press This piece of equipment is used to cover button molds with top cover. However, it is not essential, since many sewing machine shops and upholsterers offer a covering service.

Tool tray Have a plastic or wooden tray with compartments and a handle to hold your tools, and a roll of soft cloth to hold needles and skewers.

C-Clamp This can be used to clamp slip seat frames to trestles.

Other items Have on hand a variety of plastic lids and other small containers for storing tacks and pins.

A note pad and pencil are useful for reminders about the work: measurements, buttoning patterns, etc, which are so easily forgotten. I also use a camera to keep records of my work. A supply of envelopes can be used for storing screws that are removed and that can be replaced (make a note of where they have come from).

You will need chalk for marking measurements.

Disposable gauze masks should be used when you are removing dusty materials from old upholstery.

Finally, to keep your workspace neat, have a dustpan and brush, a vacuum cleaner, and large bags for trash.

A pair of high trestles based on a design such as this will make your work a great deal easier. The dimensions given will help you to plan your own design.

Upholstery Tools

Because most work on traditional upholstery involves the removal of dilapidated materials, the taking-down tools are listed first, although of course in practice most tools are multi-purpose.

TAKING-DOWN TOOLS

Ripping chisel Used with a wooden mallet for removing tacks (p65), it is available with straight or crooked shanks. I find the crooked shank best purely as a tack remover (I file it just a little finer, but not so much that it cuts into materials that I want to save). I use the straight-shanked chisel as an aid when tacking into awkward spots (p66) and as a lever.

Wooden mallet Square carpenter's mallets (for use with the ripping chisel) are available in various sizes, so find one that is comfortable for you. Cylindrical carver's mallets can also be used. I have had two cylindrical-headed mallets made for me by a wood-turner that are smaller than the standard ones, and I find them very comfortable to use, well balanced, and work-effective.

Tack lifter In spite of its name, this tool is not much used for tacks, but to remove decorative nails.

Utility knife A sharp knife is essential for cutting up old materials and twines and for various trimming tasks. Have a generous supply of new blades – they blunt surprisingly quickly on tough old fabrics. For safety use the type with a fixed blade.

Scissors will also be useful for cutting away old fabrics.

Pliers and pincers These are used for hauling out stubborn materials and old nails from the frame. The pliers illustrated are useful for general work. Pincers, with rounded ends, will give a firmer and more accurate grip.

Wire cutters I find a small pair with pointed blades invaluable for digging out stubborn tacks.

REBUILDING TOOLS

Hammers Regarded as the archetypal upholsterer's tools, the claw hammer and two-headed hammer are used for general work; the cabriole hammer (smaller and lighter in weight) is used for work that demands great care, such as tacking near show wood.

Choose a hammer with a magnetic head to allow you to pick up and position tacks without the danger of hitting fingers and thumbs, and also to free your hand to hold the fabrics. It may seem to present additional difficulties at first, the head bristling porcupine style with unwanted tacks, but with practice you will soon be able to pick up individual tacks (p66) and work at speed. Buy the best.

Webbing stretcher This is probably the only upholstery tool that has just one function, and it is absolutely essential. Never be tempted to pull webbing taut by hand, for it will inevitably sag.

There are several types of webbing stretcher. The slot and peg type illustrated is the one I use, but in the United States you are more likely to find the rubber-ended type. This has a grooved strip of rubber at one end (placed against the chair frame) and a row of spikes at the other, over which the webbing is fastened.

Steel jaw hide strainer Used mainly for straining hide top cover, it can also be used to grip short ends of webbing.

Needles You will need a variety of these, described on p54.

Scissors Have at least two pairs: a large pair for cutting top cover, muslin, and burlap, and a pair with small pointed blades for snipping into awkward corners and for cutting threads.

Sharpen them regularly and avoid cutting into tacks on materials to prevent damage to the blades.

Adhesives Water-based adhesive is used for gluing gimp. Scotch tape is useful for binding the ends of cords and gimps while working, and for removing fluff.

Measures I find four types useful at different times: a flexible tape measure because I can drape it around my neck when not in use; a retractable steel tape for measuring very large pieces; a yardstick or steel ruler (used with a try square). invaluable when cutting out top cover; and a short wooden or steel ruler to use as a gauge for edges.

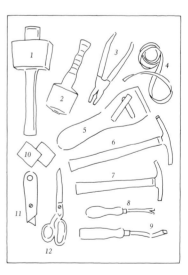

1 carpenter's mallet 2 handmade cylindrical-headed mallet 3 pliers 4 tape measure 5 slot and peg webbing stretcher 6 double-headed magnetic hammer 7 magnetic claw hammer 8 tack lifter 9 ripping chisel 10 tailor's chalk 11 utility knife 12 scissors

Upholstery Materials

Webbing Black and white "English" herringbone webbing is the sturdiest and should always be used for seats. It is made from woven cotton and flax. Brown jute webbing can be used on backs and arms.

Webbing is sold by the roll or by length. The most useful width is 5cm/2in.

Burlap Made from jute, burlap is fixed over the webbing and/or springs to form the basic support. The heavier the weight the better the quality – always use the best available for the base.

Heavyweight burlap (also called spring canvas) must be used on all sprung seats, backs and arms to withstand the friction of the springs, and on large seats of all types.

Medium-weight burlap is suitable for seats with light use and the inside backs and arms of most work.

Lightweight burlap should be used only for backs and arms that will have light use. Never use it as a seat base burlap.

Scrim This loosely-woven cotton or linen fabric is used to cover the first stuffing before stitching the pad; the loose weave of the strong jute fibers allows the stuffing to be regulated through it to mold the required shape.

Muslin Strong unbleached muslin is used to cover the pad before top covering. Unlike burlaps, which have gradations of quality to suit different purposes, anything less than the best in muslin has nothing to recommend it, so please give your careful work a well-lined jacket.

Bottom lining This black fabric, usually cambric, is used to cover the underside of sprung seats to give a neat finish and to catch the dust. Another term for it is "dustcatcher."

Many upholsterers bottom-line all seats, although historically the practice dates only from 19th-century sprung seating. Use only good quality lining; the cheap version is so thin and unpleasant that it is difficult to work with and gives a shoddy finish.

Alternatively, use muslin or decking to match the top cover.

Decking This is a sturdy denim fabric used for the deck of a chair – that is, for a seat that will be fitted with a cushion. It helps you to economize on top cover and, with its matte surface, provides a non-slip surface for cushions covered in slippery fabrics.

Waxed cambric Used as a casing to house cushion feathers. One side of this fabric is waxed to prevent them from piercing through.

Back tacking strip A thin strip of fibrous material used to give a straight edge to the top cover tack line if not covered in braid or gimp. As an alternative, use a strip of webbing, cut in half lengthwise.

Buckram Cloth stiffened with size, used to define corners.

Batting The function of batting is to provide a thin softening layer between the muslin and top cover.
Polyester batting This is readily available in several thicknesses. A thickness of about 1cm/½in is the most useful for general use.
Cotton batting This is denser and less springy than polyester. Choose the kind that has a "skin" on one side, which keeps the fibers from moving, and always choose the best quality.
Felted cotton Also called cotton felt or linterfelt, this soft padding (resembling a coarse absorbent cotton) is used mainly as a thin stuffing or as an additional top filler; it is also used as padding

under the top cover.

Stuffings Unfortunately, the best stuffing, 100 percent horsehair (which curls to produce a wonderful springy, firm, and comfortable padding), is no longer generally available. However, if you find horsehair in an old chair that you are reupholstering, you may be able to re-use it.
Curled hair Made of 50 percent horsehair and 50 percent hog hair, this is the closest equivalent in the United States to traditional horsehair.
Grey hair This is made of short animal hairs (often hog hair), which cannot be curled. It is found in Britain.
Polished black fiber This vegetable fiber is also available in Britain and is a reasonable substitute for horsehair, particularly as a first stuffing. Although obviously not as good, its long, curling fibers have a springy resilience and durability.

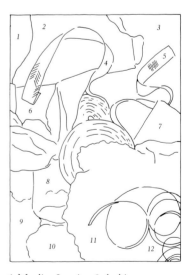

1 *Muslin* 2 *scrim* 3 *decking*
4/5 *webbing* 6 *burlap*
7 *polyester batting* 8 *cotton batting*
9 *polished black fiber* 10 *grey hair*
11 *felted cotton* 12 *back tacking strip*

Fixings and Springs

Cords, threads, and twines You will need to have a variety handy in your toolbox.

Laid cord Made from hemp or jute, this stout cord is used to lash springs together onto the frame. Never be tempted to use a substitute for this task.

Stitching twine Used for stitching throughout the making of upholstery pads.

Nylon twine Generally used to tie off buttons. I also use it to stitch springs to the webbing and base burlap, as it is so strong.

Strong linen thread This is used for slipstitching medium-weight top cover.

Waxed carpet thread Available in skeins of different colors, it is also used for slipstitching top covers and sewing trimming cord.

Machine-stitching threads The type and strength of thread used for stitching top covers and cushions should be selected according to the weight and type of fabric being used.

Needles Have a good selection of the wide range available.

Regulators Indispensable aids for numerous situations, they are used primarily to distribute (or "regulate") the stuffing evenly.

I usually have two or three of these at hand; the medium size is the most useful.

Straight (mattress) needles These are used to stitch edges, to insert stuffing ties, and for buttoning.

Round-pointed needles are used for normal work, and bayonet-pointed needles (with squared points) will cut through tough materials on heavy work.

I find 25cm/10in, 30cm/12in and 36cm/14in the most useful lengths.

Spring needles Curved, bayonet-pointed needles, usually 13cm/5in long, they are used to stitch springs to webbing and burlap.

Curved needles Equip yourself with a selection of different sizes. They are used for different kinds of stitching from fine slipstitching of top cover to heavier work, such as bridle ties.

Upholstery pins Used for temporarily fixing materials, these are larger and stronger than the dressmaker's variety, although I keep a supply of the latter for working on fine top cover.

Skewers Serving the same purpose as pins, they are longer and stronger and used for heavier work.

Tacks Have a wide selection available for use. They are made in a great range of lengths, all the way from No. 1($\frac{3}{16}$in) to No. 24 (1$\frac{1}{8}$in). The width increases slightly along with the length. For most purposes you will find sizes 3 to 10 the most useful. The recommendations given here are for general guidance, but you must consider the size and condition of the tack rail as well as the material and the wear it will receive.

No. 2 tacks are for very delicate work and are rarely used.

No. 3 tacks are used mainly for muslin and top covering.

No. 4 tacks are for top covering with heavy fabrics and for attaching scrim or burlap to light rails.

No. 6 tacks are for very heavy top covers, for tacking through several layers, and for webbing that will receive light use.

No. 8 tacks are for webbing, if the tack rail necessitates, and for attaching base burlap.

No. 10 tacks are for webbing on medium- to heavyweight rails and for attaching base burlap to large frames.

Gimp pins As their name implies these slender tacks are used for finishing work on gimps, braids, and top covers, but they are also useful in other situations where very fine-headed tacks are required (such as at gathers in muslin around arms when layers of wider tack heads would block the rail and make tacking the top cover very difficult).

Decorative nails The most commonly used are shiny brass-plated steel dome-headed nails. They are also available in a dull antique finish, but I prefer to wait for the bright ones to tarnish naturally.

You will find a wide variety of high-quality decorated and shaped nails, both bright and antique, if you inquire at a good fabric store.

Springs Double-cone springs for traditional upholstery are available in several heights, designated by the number of coils above the center, which ranges from 1 to 5. Springs also vary in the gauge, or thickness, of the wire used, which determines their degree of stiffness.

Edge wire This is used to reinforce the front edge of sprung pads (p93 and p154).

*1 tacks **2** double-cone spring **3** nylon twine **4** lashing cord **5** stitching twine **6** pins **7** skewers **8** straight needles **9** spring needle **10** curved needles **11** regulators **12** brass nails **13** gimp pins*

Fabrics

By the time your chair or sofa is upholstered and ready for top covering, you will understand its spirit, and your instinct for what is "right" will guide your choice of fabric. During the process of taking it down, creating a shape with stuffing, and emphasizing the line with trimming or nailing, allow your thoughts to turn to top cover fabrics.

Give imagination free rein as you contemplate your transformed chair in its setting, or even rethink your room decoration to suit it. Indulge in a fantasy of textures and moods, colors and designs. Wander down paths festooned with silks and velvets, slubby linens, romantic moirés, and lustrous damasks – heavy with colors, crisp with stripes, frothy with pattern. But be sure to come down to earth before making your final choice, for some important factors must be taken into account.

Top covering a chair or sofa may be compared to dressing a person – preferences for color, pattern, and texture on the one hand, and practicalities such as function, durability, and cost on the other. The fabric must also suit the wearer: you would hardly dress an elegant lady of mature years and refined disposition in a razzle-dazzle party skirt. Equally, a plumply buttoned boudoir chair, turning a pretty ankle through draped skirts, will not best be suited in sober gray flannel. Trimmings, too, need to be chosen with all the care you would bring to finding the right accessories for a special outfit.

The period style of the piece may well be a consideration when searching for a top cover. You may want a fabric that is identical or similar to the original one. In restoration this is an important factor, and where true authenticity is sought and a remnant of the original top cover is found on the frame, a length of fabric can be woven to match. The expense is justifiable for rare and important pieces. Most of us, however, have to compromise, and there is a wide range of modern equivalents based on traditional designs to be found.

Sometimes, too, you may be lucky enough to find sufficient quantities of an old material that is sympathetic to the original. Awareness of what the original fabric was like may do no more than give you a clue as to the kind of patterning or textural effect you want to apply to your chair – a hint of the "spirit" of the fabric you are looking for. But it can nevertheless provide you with an excellent starting point in your search for the right fabric.

Above all, the fabric should be one *you* like. Remember that when the chairs were new, their covers suited the owner's personal taste, requirements, and purse, as well as the fashion of the time. These criteria should still apply: if the fabric enhances the chair and the room as well as giving you lasting pleasure, then it is well chosen.

Preferences and Practicalities

If the upholstery is sound and firmly jacketed in good muslin, the top cover can be replaced if it becomes dirty or worn – or ceases to please you. However, do bear in mind that every time this is done the

Some designs seem to survive across all cultures through the ages. These powerful patterns are still finding uses in modern upholstery.
1 *Bold use of velvet on silk for a striking and aggressive effect.*
2 *An intricate 16th-century Italian design in silk damask.*
3 *A design adapted from part of the border panel of an Elizabethan bedhanging now in the Victoria & Albert Museum, London.*
4 *Vibrant, deep colors feature in rich, complex patterns in this design.*
5 *Traditional damask is used for this subdued design, originally dating from the 19th century.*
6 *These deep red and dark greens were popular decorating colors for the late Victorian interior. The design is taken from* The Grammar of Ornament, *by Owen Jones, published in 1856.*
7 *A distinct Indian influence can be seen in this printed design, taken from the cover of a late-19th-century* chaise longue.
8 *Intricate damask weaving in delicately colored silk creates an elegant effect.*
9 *Dating from about 1930, this design features cotton and wool embroidered on tapestry-quality damask.*
10 *A Renaissance-inspired design in printed cotton.*
11 *Iridescent silk moiré with self-patterned dots woven in.*
12 *This wool fabric is based on a 5th-century Egyptian design woven originally in silk.*

1

2

3

4

5

6

7

8

9

11

12

frame is subjected to the heavy physical assault of removing and renewing tacks, which is particularly damaging to old chairs. So, in addition to aesthetic preferences, it is important to consider the fabric's practical function, the particular combination of fiber, weave, and finish that gives it textural identity and determines its wearing properties.

The manufacturers' "wear codes" will help you base your choice on practicalities as well as looks. You will need to think about where the chair is to be kept and who will be using it. The family with a sticky-fingered toddler would be ill-advised to cover a chair in palest buttermilk-colored moiré, unless it is to be kept in a private boudoir.

You will want the look and feel of the fabric to suit both the chair and its surroundings, as well as its function. Fibers such as wool and plain weaves in thicker cotton or linen are matte-textured, whereas a smooth satin-weave cotton or silk, the glaze of a chintz, and the directional nap of velvet all catch the light. The contrast between the highlighted and shaded areas of such fabrics will accentuate the contours in the upholstery and can be exploited to enhance the shaping. Incidentally, these smooth fabrics often convey a more opulent and luxurious mood than the lower-key plain weaves.

Surface texture influences the quality of color in a fabric. Artificial light, too, can change our perception of color. If you are likely to use your chair most in the evenings, leave a large sample draped over it for a few days so that you can see how different light affects the tones, and whether the fabric harmonizes with other colors in the room.

Pattern, too, contributes to the impact of a fabric. Its scale should be considered in relation to the style and size of the chair. Although I do not subscribe to the theory that anything more than a small all-over pattern is wasted on a buttoned chair, it is obvious that a bold motif with a deep drop would be obscured in a mass of buttoning. A large design is shown to best effect running down, almost unbroken, on the inside back and the seat of a plain sofa or large armchair. Make sure that the panels show the pattern to best advantage. Remember, too, that stripes tend to elongate a shape, and that unpatterned fabric makes large surfaces look bigger. It is more difficult to work with a subtly figured pattern than one with clearly contrasting motifs or shapes that "read" distinctly at a distance. Repeats can easily be matched or balanced.

Unfortunately, cost is usually a deciding factor in your choice, for upholstery fabrics are expensive. Force yourself to pay a little more than you think you can afford. The quality will be better, the range more extensive, you will be happier with it – and you will have forgotten all about the expense by the time you are sitting on your newly restored chair!

Traditional Fabrics

The abundance of reproduction fabrics offers you a good chance of dressing a chair in something remarkably similar to its original covering. Certain fabrics have remained furnishing "classics," perhaps

Delicately colored patterns have long been popular in upholstery fabric design, and some achieve a rare beauty and subtlety.

1 An elegant woven design based on a cross stitch pattern.

2 This printed cotton design is the epitome of the English flower print.

3 A dream-like maze of ribbon, knots, and bows, printed on glazed cotton.

4 The influence of Venetian motifs is apparent in this printed cotton design.

5 A trellis design full of rhythm and contrast.

6 A printed cotton design based on the avant-garde *freehand patterns of the 1920s.*

7 A fine brocade in the Italian tradition with a flowered stripe alternating with a delicate plaid.

8 A striking, naturalistic image based on an 18th-century chinoiserie design.

9 A subtle design in moiré silk.

10 This design is copied from an 1840s cotton print discovered on a valance. Simple floral patterns were the mainstay of textile production in the first half of the 19th century. The trellis overgrown with rosebuds is a pattern characteristic of the period.

11 A strong French influence can be seen in this silk woven design from Spitalfields, London, dated 1880. It is reproduced here in woven cotton.

12 Originally produced in the 1950s, this design uses the classic toile de Jouy coloring which came from the natural dye, madder.

2

3

5

6

7

8

9

11

12

nowadays slightly modified and incorporating modern dyes and fibers in their make-up. Velvets, for instance, in silk, cotton, and acrylic are plentiful in a wide range of weights, shades, and textures. Woven horsehair or haircloth, both patterned and plain, is available, although expensive. Leather, that time-honored alternative to textiles, is still easily available.

Although textures and colors are not always exactly reproduced by modern looms, fibers, and dyes, many beautiful fabrics are now made that faithfully copy the designs of previous centuries. Printed fabrics, in particular, offer a tremendously broad range of original designs. Copies of 18th- and 19th-century chintzes are available at reasonable prices, and many designs, originated by the Arts and Crafts Movement, Art Nouveau, Liberty, and so on, continue to be made. Some up-to-date effects successfully emulate outmoded printing techniques or imitate patterns originally achieved by weaving processes.

Many woven designs also draw on period inspiration. There are damasks and brocades in authentic designs or simply with a traditional feel. Tapestry fabrics today are intended to create a period flavor of needlework and tapestry covers.

New Fabric Designs

Contemporary fabrics can look very exciting on old furniture, and, whatever the setting, may help the chair or sofa look appropriate even in high tech surroundings. No one should be denied the joy and comfort of the curves and swells of tradition.

One course to take is to opt for a contemporary adaptation of the period design – one that reinterprets it in today's idiom. Instead of an all-over traditional flowery chintz, you could choose a swirling modern pattern of flowers and leaves, or break further away and go for a soft-edged abstract repeating pattern. Instead of formal woven damask with its figured design, a two-toned printed pattern could convey a similar feel. Instead of crisp, clearly defined stripes, you could choose an ikat weave with a blurred linear effect, or a printed version with a subtle directional quality. Good fabric design, like good upholstery, will grow old gracefully.

Using Old Materials

One way of giving a chair or sofa a "new" top cover that has an indefinably mature and interesting character is by recycling old fabrics. This may make you a financial saving, but its greatest advantage is that your fabric will have the unique patina of age. Old velvet curtains, faded bronze with age and light, will gently cloak strong, resilient new upholstery, creating a mood of tranquility. Look for shawls, rugs, hangings, and bedcovers in antique shops and markets. Kelim rugs look superb on ottomans, footstools, and sofas, and on armchairs with large smooth surfaces.

First check for quantity: old materials are usually found in short lengths, but seeming miracles can be worked if you are prepared to spend the extra time in cutting and fitting, especially in buttoned

Geometric and abstract designs revel in the use of patterns that do not mirror nature, but draw on its influence to create entirely new images.

1 A two-color jacquard weave in thick upholstery-weight cotton with a brocade finish.

2 An abstract two-color design in printed cotton.

3 Called "Venezia Carnivale," this printed cotton design evokes the atmosphere of Venice at carnival time.

4 Turkish kelim motifs inspired this tapestry weave of jagged stripes.

5 This French design in lightly glazed cotton features multi-colored speckles and dashes on a colored background.

6 This highly geometric pattern was derived from a 19th-century design held in the Victoria & Albert Museum, London.

7 A complex design of roses, lightly delineated in gold, sketched on richly patterned stripes.

8 An elegant design using two shades of green to make a fluid pattern.

9 Clean vertical lines on a soft blue patterned background create a striking effect.

10 This design, based on linoleum, incorporates abstract cyclamen shapes in its weave.

11 A pastel bouclé design called "Marisol."

12 Plaids and stripes are favorites with some designers for their striking but elegant patterns.

2

3

5

6

8

9

11

12

work (p110), and with the use of extension flies (p108). Next check for strength. The fabric may be worn and flawed in places. If you cannot avoid using these areas, position them on the outside, where they will be relatively safe. The fabric must, however, be strong enough to withstand the tension when fitting, especially when buttoning. If you suspect that it might not, then it is probably incapable of standing reasonable wear anyway.

Trimmings

The piece is virtually complete by the time any gimp and so on is applied, yet it is astonishing how much difference this seemingly inconsequential detail can have on the overall effect. Although trimmings may seem like finishing touches, they should not be afterthoughts. They need to harmonize in style and mood with the chosen fabric, and with the style of the chair, particularly if it is a "period classic." Consider them early, in the same careful way that you contemplate the top cover fabrics. Some trimming materials, such as piping, are sewn into the top cover before it is fixed to the frame, and are an integral part of the whole. Some are necessary cover-ups for seams and tacks, while others are pure decoration.

Old trimmings will be more in keeping with antique materials, but you will probably have to buy new ones. You could dip them in in weak black coffee or tea to "age" them – do a small test sample first.

Piping, cord, and rope all serve as outlining, emphasizing shape. Piping (which is sewn into the seams of the top cover) is formal and streamlined; in a contrasting color or texture, it can add a touch of drama; or it can simply add a discreet interest. Cords and ropes are sewn onto the top-covered chair and create a fuller, more sumptuous look than piping. I confess to being a cord fetishist and use them coiled and knotted, curved, looped, and swathed.

Gimp is used mainly to cover tacks. These loosely woven narrow bands are both functional and decorative. Wisely chosen, they will enhance your top cover and accentuate the lines of the frame.

Braids are tightly woven flat bands which are stitched onto top cover panels (often in squares or rectangles around inside backs, for example) for decoration and accentuation of shape.

Fringe can be simple and lightweight or ornately tasseled; it is made from a wide range of fibers. (The best selection can be found in Europe – a fact worth bearing in mind if you're planning a trip there.) Consider using a fringe along arms and tops of outside backs, as well as in its usual role as a skirt finish to the seat. There is also a kind of looped fringe, called ruche, which is sewn into seams for decoration and emphasis. Fringes are available in standard measurements; special lengths can be made to order but are costly. Clever placing on the frame can overcome problems of length, or a pair of fringes (a short one above a matching longer one, or a trellis above a longer bullion one) may give the right effect.

Tassels, whether tiny and tantalizing or fat and frothy, make a bold statement and are not for the faint-hearted. I love to see them dangling from strategic points of upholstery, cushions, and bolsters, serving no function other than to entertain.

Many department stores and upholstery suppliers offer a range of trimmings that can be used for upholstery work. There are also specialists that stock a wide variety of lavish trimmings, a selection of which is shown here. The large tassels and rope are sold as drapery tiebacks; the smaller ones are key tassels. Other trimmings from top to bottom:
Braid
Gimp
Fringe
Gimp
Fancy gimp
Braid
Tasseled fringe
Cord piping
Ruche
Fanned fringe
Tasseled fringe

Pin-stuffed pad

Stuffed pad with finger-roll edges

Double-stuffed stitched pad

Double-stuffed stitched pad with sprung base

Pleat-tufted pad with stitched edge

Upholstery Techniques

This section takes you through all the processes of traditional upholstery techniques, from the basic information that is required for every project, through the special techniques for upholstery pads (graduating from the simplest pin stuffing to the complexities of pleated tufting), to the making of cushions and the final top covering. It will provide you with an information "kit" or directory of techniques and styles that can be applied to any work that you tackle. The projects on pp116–181 show how I have put these processes into practice and demonstrate by example how they can be adapted.

It is important to realize that each technical procedure creates a different shape and each has its own individual properties of durability and comfort which must be related to the size of the frame and its use. For instance, to form a thin, flat pin-stuffed pad on a frame that is clearly designed for a deeply sprung stitched pad would obviously not support the sitter in a comfortable position. Give thought to the depth of the pads: arms should be the correct height for resting elbows; inside backs should not be so deep that they shorten the seat and project the sitter forward.

Remember that upholstery has to withstand aggressive treatment. The impact of weight and stress of a person sitting on a seat is repeated every time it is used. It is therefore vital to build a firm foundation, and to work right through to muslin stage, paying attention to every detail. Sloppy work and "make do" dodges always come to grief in use.

Start with a simple project if you are a beginner – a slip seat (p116), for instance. If you cannot find a suitable piece of furniture you could make a simple square wooden frame on which to practice. Familiarize yourself with some basic rules and tips on how to use the tools, the order of working, and so on. Practice the simple tasks first and gain confidence with your tools and materials. Take each step quietly and don't worry if things go wrong. Just take out the work and try again. If you seem to hit a bad patch and just cannot get it right, leave it for a few hours, or even a few days. You will understand the problem clearly and calmly when you return to it refreshed, and work that had been a demon, fighting you at every stage, will again become an amenable companion.

Planning the work

Having decided on the project, you must now do some forward planning. If you are working on a new frame you will have to decide on the shape of your upholstery and measure for the basic materials accordingly. Top cover and trimmings may be considered before you start work, or you may choose to respond to the spirit of the chair as you work on it and make your choice when it is finished.

If the frame is an old one that has been stripped of all existing materials you should first check the soundness of the frame. This is done by standing in front of the chair or sofa with one knee resting on the front of the seat; with both hands gently pull first on one inside back rail and then on the other. Any give at the arm or seat rail joints is an indication of trouble; the joints should be repaired and all upholstery, however sound, will usually have to be removed.

If you are re-making or repairing existing upholstery you must not only examine the frame but also judge the state of the upholstery. A simple repair or new top cover may be all that is required. For total re-upholstery you will need to remove or "take down" all existing materials and start from scratch. If this is the case you will have to decide whether you are going to re-create the existing shape (in which case you should photograph the work and make a note of any details you will need for future reference) or to change it. For instance, a chair with a smooth back could be pleat-tufted (p8).

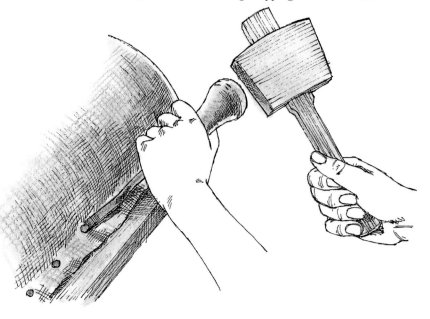

Using a ripping chisel and mallet

Taking down

This is also known as "ripping out," a destructive term that I hate, but that nonetheless conveys the nature of this aggressive task. Taking down requires brute force, and, at times, dogged perseverance in order to work free stubborn tacks and well-lashed knots.

A professional upholsterer will usually cut and haul away as much worn upholstery as possible and then "clean" the frame of tacked materials, using the tools that are listed on p50. However, you will learn much more about upholstery techniques if you remove each layer individually and note the construction, particularly if you intend to re-upholster in the same manner. You may also be able to re-use some of the materials (particularly the stuffing) if they are in good condition.

Use a ripping chisel and mallet to remove tacks from the frame. It is a strenuous operation: lodge the chisel under the head of the tack and strike it with a sharp blow as you flick the chisel upward. Work in the direction of the grain of the wood to avoid splitting and weakening the frame.

Start underneath the seat with the bottom lining (p113), if there is one, then make checks to judge whether your chair needs only to be re-covered. If it is covered in muslin, run your hands over the upholstery to ensure that it is firm and does not

sag, particularly at the front edge of the seat and arms. If a stitched edge can be "rocked," or is flattened or otherwise distorted, it must be re-made. Now turn the chair upside down and peer through the webbing and stitched springs to check the condition of the base burlap. It should not be frayed at areas of extreme stress, for instance, at the points of contact with the springs and the edge of the front seat rail. If you are satisfied that all is sound, a new top cover can be fitted. If you have any doubts at all, remove the upholstery – there is no point in spending money and effort to re-cover doubtful upholstery.

Beneath the muslin you will come to the top stuffing and/or the

stuffing pad, where you will find one of a variety of materials.

Horsehair, the most likely to survive, can be removed and put aside for re-use in its complete form if the pad is sound and smooth. If it is lumpy you can tease it back into springy mounds by pulling all the strands apart and discarding any knots; better still, put the whole lot in an old pillow case tied firmly at the opening and handwash and spin dry it before teasing the stuffing.

A stuffing pad filled with wood shavings falls apart on removal and must be discarded. Ginger fiber and sea grasses can sometimes be re-used, but if they are short and crumbling they must be discarded.

If the stitched pads are fairly

sound they can be removed intact and put aside for re-use. They can be re-positioned on new base work, covered with a new scrim and re-stitched. There is no virtue in discarding a perfectly good pad to make a new one.

Continue to remove all the upholstery, discarding all worn materials (unless they are of particular interest and you want to preserve them for reference). Make a note of the buttoning patterns and springing patterns if you wish to re-create them. Springs can be re-used only if they are straight and firm.

Using a magnetic hammer

Basic rules and tips

Tools Using the correct tools in the correct way will save both time and energy and improve your results. Take time to become familiar with them, and take advantage of their versatility: a regulator, for instance, is invaluable in many situations.

Grasp hammers at the end of the handle, to give more accurate aim and greater impact with less effort. Do not point the index finger down the shaft – it is not a dinner knife! Use a magnetic hammer and

practice picking up individual tacks.

If you are tacking into an awkward spot that the hammer will not reach, lodge the tack in the rail. Pushing the tack with your fingers, hold the tip of a straight chisel to the top of the tack and knock the handle of the chisel with the flat of your hammer head.

A regulator is used primarily to "regulate" or adjust stuffing. Insert the pointed end at an angle and to the depth required. Sweep it around

to fill dips and smooth lumps.

A regulator can also be used as an extra "finger" when tacking to difficult rails.

This useful tool will also prove handy for working fabric between pads where your fingers cannot reach. Stitch a twine through the fabric with a needle, then thread both ends through the eye of the regulator, push it through the awkward space, and pull the twines to draw the fabric through.

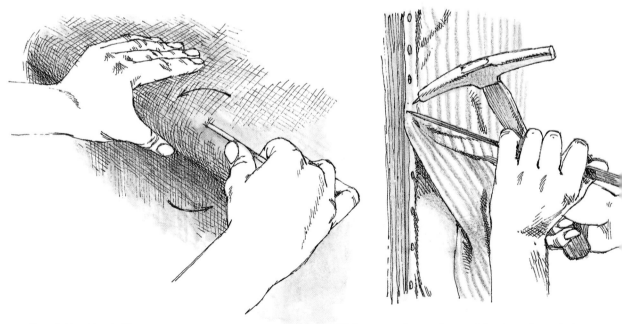

Regulating the stuffing

Using a regulator when tacking in awkward places

Materials Make a generous allowance when cutting materials until you have gained confidence in working. I recommend 8cm/3in on all sides for base materials, and a 5cm/2in allowance for top cover (p106). In time you will be able to reduce the quantities specified in the instructions.

Order of working There are three basic rules to consider.
1 When planning your work it is generally advisable to start with the inside back, then do the arms, seat, and finally the outside back. However, if you are working on a complicated piece, such as a wing chair or chesterfield, you may prefer to work the seat at an early stage so that you have a surface to rest your tools on.
2 In general it is wise to work the back and front rails before the sides, but you should always start by working on the rails that determine the shape of the chair.
3 Always work on rails from the center out toward the sides. When working on webs, start by fixing the center web. Either complete one side and then the other, or work on both sides alternately.

When working with fabrics, fold the materials to find the center, place at the center of the rail, and tack at this point first, then fix one tack on either side. On straight rails work to one side and then the other. On curves and other shapes work alternately on either side of the center to make sure that any patterns are symmetrical, that the cloth is "set square," and that any "cleaning" (the cutting away of waste material) occurs at the corners or end of rails.

Squaring the fabrics It is vital that all materials such as webbings, scrims, muslins, and top cover be always fixed square to the frame in order to take advantage of their strength and durability. Train yourself from the start automatically to follow threads by eye and tack off warp and weft threads square. This habit will help you when tacking materials over three-dimensional shapes, pulling them over smoothly and evenly, especially when it comes to working with top cover.

To ensure accuracy, you can use the point of a regulator to pull the fabric forward (in line with the tacks on the opposite rail) and pin it to the frame to hold it in place while you tack.

If you tack the fabric too tightly it will strain across the pad and create a tension line, known as a "tack tie." To correct this, release the fabric and re-tack correctly.

Tension The tension of materials must be sound and regular in order to distribute weight and wear evenly. This is something that you will learn to judge instinctively, and I have described it where necessary for each technique. In general, if the upholstery is not taut enough it will sag in use, but if it is too taut the materials will split away from the tacks and thus from the frame.

Tacking Think ahead when considering the position of tacks. This will depend on the number of layers of material and the size of the rail. If you are a beginner you should always "temporary tack" initially: bury the tack only halfway into the frame to enable removal

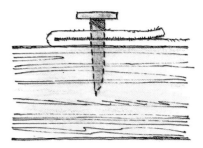

Temporary tacked

Tacked off

with a ripping chisel if it has to be repositioned.

"Tacking off" is the action of hammering the tacks home completely into the rail to anchor the fabric firmly. As you gain experience you will know which stages can be tacked off at once. Always hammer the head flat; if the heads are at an angle they will not anchor soundly and will cut through the materials.

Protecting the wood Finally, a word of caution: when working on a chair with a show wood frame, always take care to protect any vulnerable parts by wrapping them with batting, and pad your table or trestle when they are in direct contact. Show wood tack rails, which cannot usually be wrapped, should be padded when using a webbing stretcher. When close nailing near the rail, hold a piece of cardboard against rails.

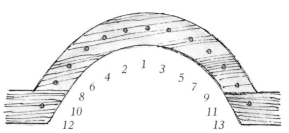

Tacking order on a straight rail and a curved rail

Knots & Stitches

Basic knots and stitches for upholstery are described and illustrated here. Once you become familiar with them you will discover their versatility and be able to use them in the way that works best for you. For instance, I generally use two or three simple half-hitch knots (shown in use opposite for a tack hold) to fasten off threads. Knots that are used for specific tasks are described with the relevant technique: bridle ties (p76), stuffing ties (p87), edge stitches (p89), spring ties, lashing, and whipping (p93).

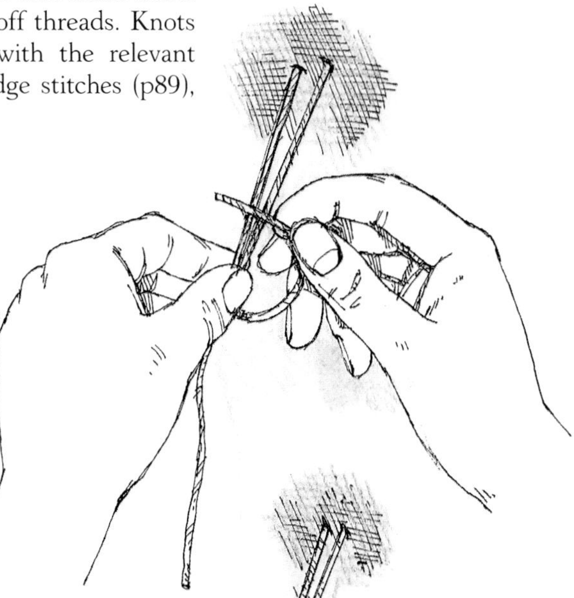

Slip knot

Slip knots are used to fasten on twines, threads, or cords that must be firmly secured or that will be under stress.

Pull the two pieces of twine or cord you are knotting toward you with your left hand, between thumb and forefinger, making sure that the short end is at least 10cm/4in long.

Loop the short end under your forefinger (a), wrap it around the two twines, and bring it back through the loop (b). Pull into a loosely tied knot (c), then pull the other twine to tighten (d).

For a double slip knot wrap the loose end twice around the other two twines.

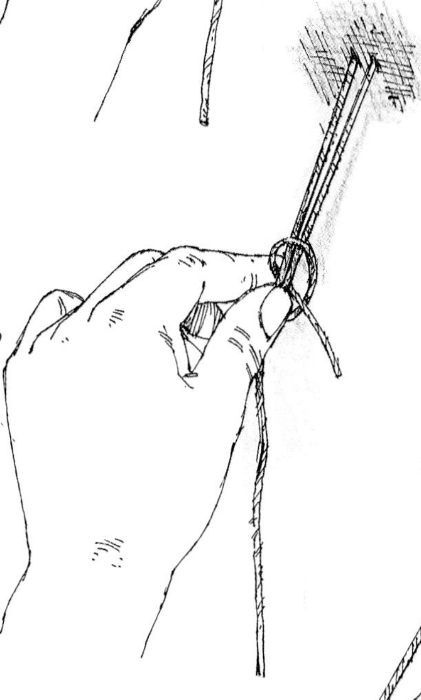

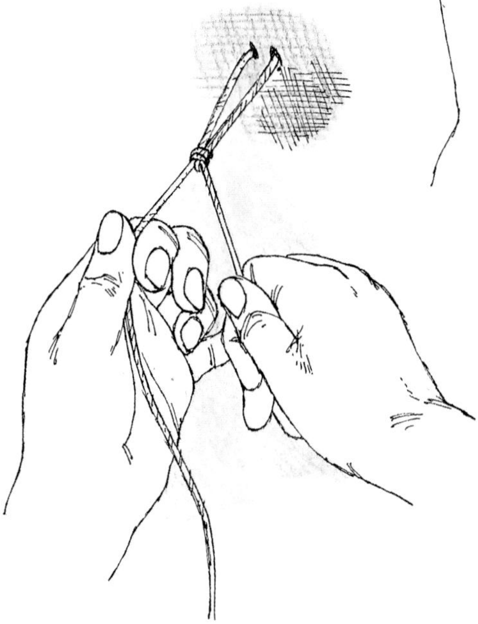

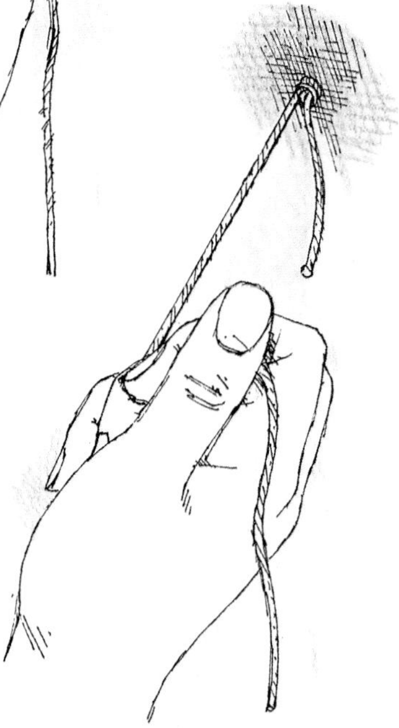

Tack hold (right)
Temporary tack a large tack into the frame. Make a half-hitch knot in a piece of twine or cord and loop it around the tack. (Alternatively, simply wind the twine around the tack.) Pull tight, and tack off firmly.

This fastening is most commonly used to secure laid cord to the frame when lashing springs (p95).

Running stitch (left)
Stitch size varies from 1cm/½in, when used to make a deck seam line (p158), to 8-10cm/3-4in for stuffing ties (p87).

Backstitch (below)
A good strong stitch for securing fabrics to one another, but it should not be used for top cover joins if they are visible.

Blanket stitch (below)
This is a useful stitch for curved joins at burlap and scrim stage (p163); pull tight to compress the stitches.

It can be used as an edge stitch to create a razor-sharp corner (p35); wind the thread around the needle twice to lock the stitch.

Slipstitch (right)
Use slipstitch for invisible seams on top cover and for sewing on cords.

To ensure that the stitches do not show, always start a stitch a couple of threads back from where the thread comes out on the other side of the seam. Pull up the threads as you work along the seam, and if the stitch shows, take it out and re-stitch.

Corners

A crisp, simple fold can be used on corners in most well-stuffed upholstery work. In the method described here the corners are worked on the front of a seat pad that is tacked to the outside rails. The opening of the folds are at the side of the seat. Indeed, wherever the corner is made, the opening of the fold should not be visible from the front of the chair. The opening can be slipstitched to neaten it, but I find this unnecessary, and prefer to see the thin shadow at the corners.

This type of corner can be made at all stages of the work and with all upholstery fabrics, from base burlap to top cover. For folds that are tacked off on the underside or back of rails, the method of working is the same.

A neat fit is important at all corners, whether they are simple folds such as these or cut around an upright rail at the corner of a pad (p122) or around a support rail at a midpoint along the edge of a pad (p134 and p141). On curved corners I work a double-fold (p125), and on some tightly curved areas, such as arm scrolls, I gather or pleat the top cover fabric to fit around the rail (p165).

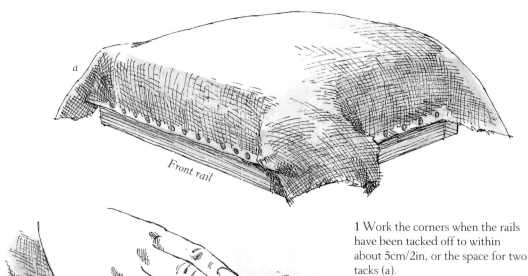

a

Front rail

b

Side rail

1 Work the corners when the rails have been tacked off to within about 5cm/2in, or the space for two tacks (a).

Turn the fabric under at the corner to align with the rest of the rail. You may need to turn under quite a lot to achieve this. (If you are tacking to the underside of the rail you will not need to turn under the edge.)

2 With your index finger, firmly wrap the fabric from the side around to the front rail and temporary tack (b).

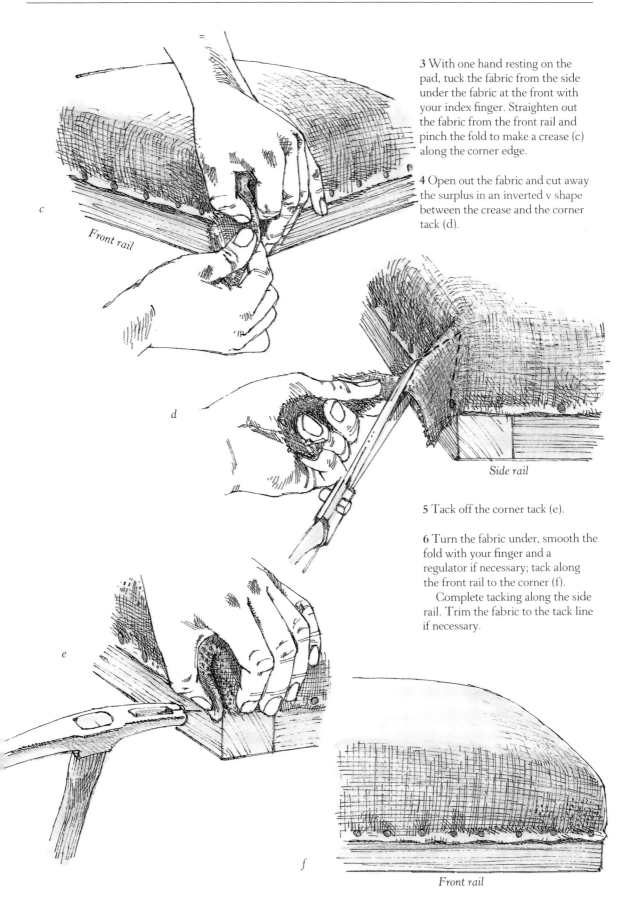

3 With one hand resting on the pad, tuck the fabric from the side under the fabric at the front with your index finger. Straighten out the fabric from the front rail and pinch the fold to make a crease (c) along the corner edge.

4 Open out the fabric and cut away the surplus in an inverted v shape between the crease and the corner tack (d).

c

Front rail

d

Side rail

5 Tack off the corner tack (e).

6 Turn the fabric under, smooth the fold with your finger and a regulator if necessary; tack along the front rail to the corner (f).

Complete tacking along the side rail. Trim the fabric to the tack line if necessary.

e

f

Front rail

Webbing

The positioning and fixing of webbing to the frame provides the support for the entire upholstery pad. It must be uniformly spaced in order to take an even distribution of weight and to give a firm base.

Select the correct webbing from the work (p52), and start working from the center of the frame rail out toward the edges, using a webbing stretcher (p50) to strain it to the opposite rail. Fix webbing to the top of seat rails and the inside of back rails for all but sprung upholstery, in which it is fixed to the underside or outside of the frame.

Webbing patterns depend not only on the upholstery method but also on shape and function: some shaped frames require a fan-like arrangement, overlapping the ends on the narrower side of the frame if necessary; webbing for sprung upholstery must be close enough to support the diameter of the springs. There are also international variations: the French style is close-webbed with no spaces between the webs.

MATERIALS
Webbing
Tacks

1 Fix the center web first. Working from the roll of webbing, turn under 2cm/¾in on the end. Place end on the top of the back rail and tack near the fold at the center; tack one on each side close to the edge. Fix two tacks alternately below to form a "w" pattern (a).

Back rail

a

2 Thread the webbing stretcher: with the cut back edge of the stretcher uppermost, fold the webbing and push it through the slot with the peg or a large nail. Insert the peg in the loop formed below (b) and pull the webbing tight to secure it.

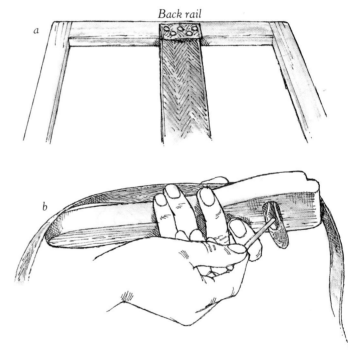
b

c

3 Grip the handle of the stretcher (together with the loose webbing) and lodge the lip of the stretcher under the edge of the front rail (protect any show wood with soft padding). Lever downward to achieve the required tension (c). To test for the correct tension, drop the head of your hammer on the web. It should bounce off, trampoline-style.

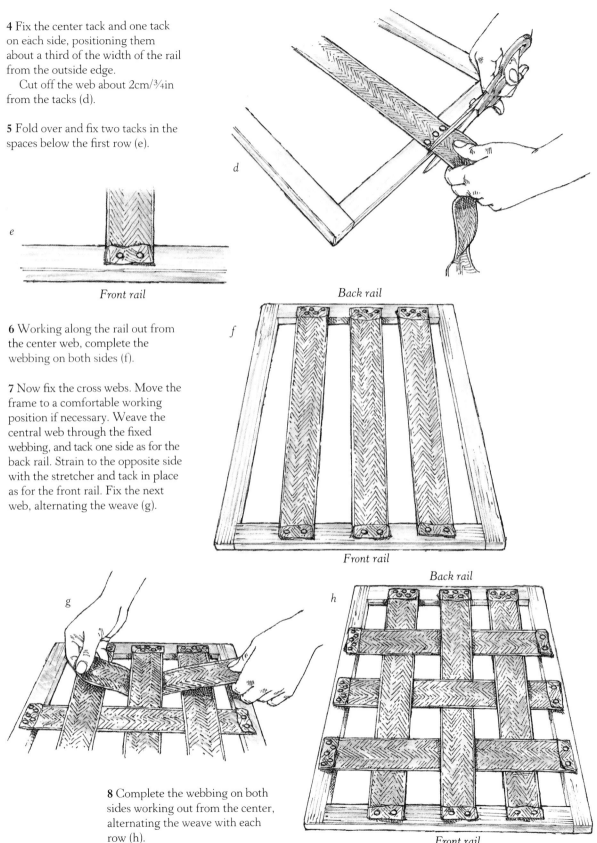

4 Fix the center tack and one tack on each side, positioning them about a third of the width of the rail from the outside edge.

Cut off the web about 2cm/¾in from the tacks (d).

5 Fold over and fix two tacks in the spaces below the first row (e).

e

Front rail

6 Working along the rail out from the center web, complete the webbing on both sides (f).

7 Now fix the cross webs. Move the frame to a comfortable working position if necessary. Weave the central web through the fixed webbing, and tack one side as for the back rail. Strain to the opposite side with the stretcher and tack in place as for the front rail. Fix the next web, alternating the weave (g).

d

Back rail

f

Front rail

g

h

Back rail

8 Complete the webbing on both sides working out from the center, alternating the weave with each row (h).

Front rail

Base Burlap

The base burlap, together with the webbing, provides the sound base upon which all subsequent layers are anchored, and therefore it is essential to create a taut and even tension.

Select the appropriate quality of burlap for the task (p52), and cut a piece about 8cm/3in larger on all sides than the frame.

For dished seats and other curved frames, make sure that you preserve the shape by working first on the rails that determine it. On iron-frame seating base burlap must be "tailored" to the correct shape and stitched to the frame (p140).

MATERIALS
Burlap
Tacks

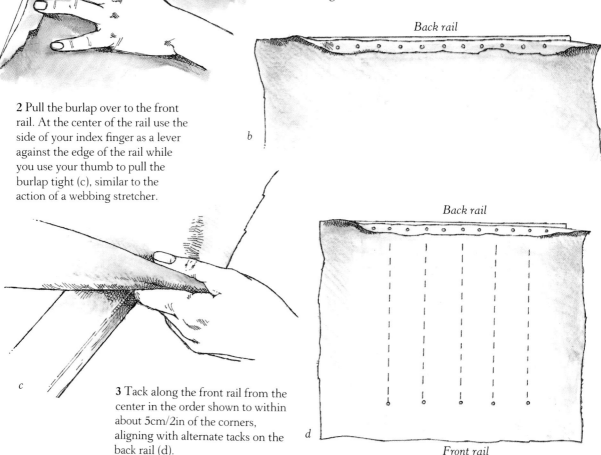

1 Start with the back rail. Turn under 2.5cm/1in and hold the burlap in position over the central web (a). Tack out from the center to within 5cm/2in of the corners at each side, following the sequence shown (b), spacing the tacks 3cm/1¼in apart, and keeping the weave straight.

Back rail

2 Pull the burlap over to the front rail. At the center of the rail use the side of your index finger as a lever against the edge of the rail while you use your thumb to pull the burlap tight (c), similar to the action of a webbing stretcher.

Back rail

3 Tack along the front rail from the center in the order shown to within about 5cm/2in of the corners, aligning with alternate tacks on the back rail (d).

Front rail

4 Work a side rail in the same way as the back rail, again turning under 2.5cm/1in (e). At the corner, pull burlap taut, fold neatly, and tack.

5 Pull fabric to the opposite side rail and attach as for the front rail (f).

6 Working on the front rail, fold over the edge (g), and tack at the midpoint between the tacks below (h). These points will correspond to the tacks on the opposite rail. (Locating the exact point to achieve an even tension can be done more accurately by using a regulator, p66.)

Tack off the unfinished side rail in the same manner (i).

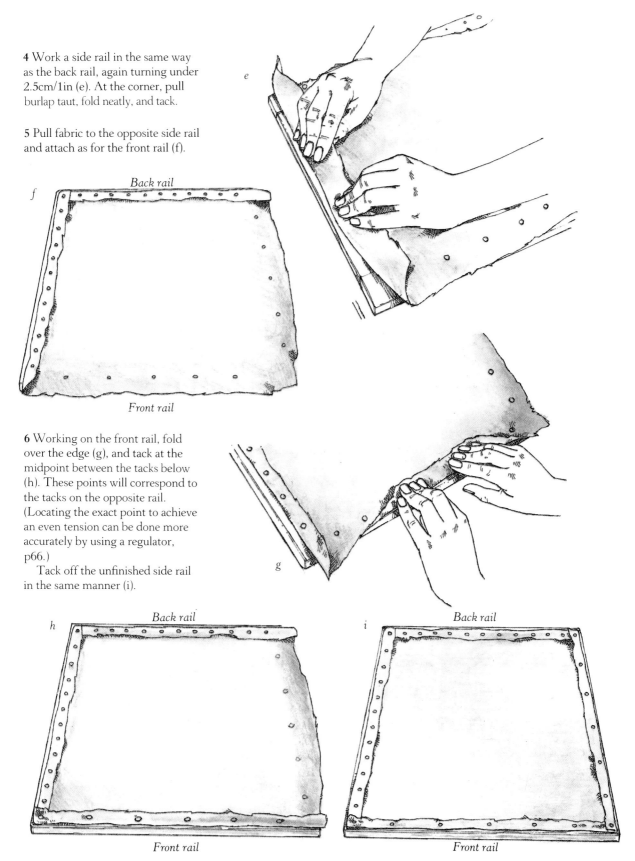

e

f *Back rail*

Front rail

g

h *Back rail*

Front rail

i *Back rail*

Front rail

75

Bridle Ties & Stuffing

Stuffing creates the depth and strength of the pad. It must be regularly distributed, with no sparse areas that make dips and without overpacking which creates lumps. It should be compact and firm enough to serve its purpose, but not so dense and solid that resilience and comfort are lost.

The depth of stuffing is controlled and held in place by bridle ties sewn into the base burlap. The continuous loops of these backstitched ties allow flexibility and can be adjusted to the depth of stuffing required. Plan the sequence of the ties to cover as much of the pad in a continuous line (right), then make any additional ties (shown by the dotted line). For a deeply stuffed edge, take the ties close to the rail; for thin stuffing, leave a space around the edge of the frame.

MATERIALS
Twine
Stuffing

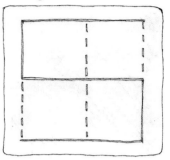

1 Before you start, examine the stuffing and pick out any "ropes" or lumps.

Thread a curved needle with a long piece of medium-weight stitching twine, and secure it near the back edge of the frame with a slip knot.

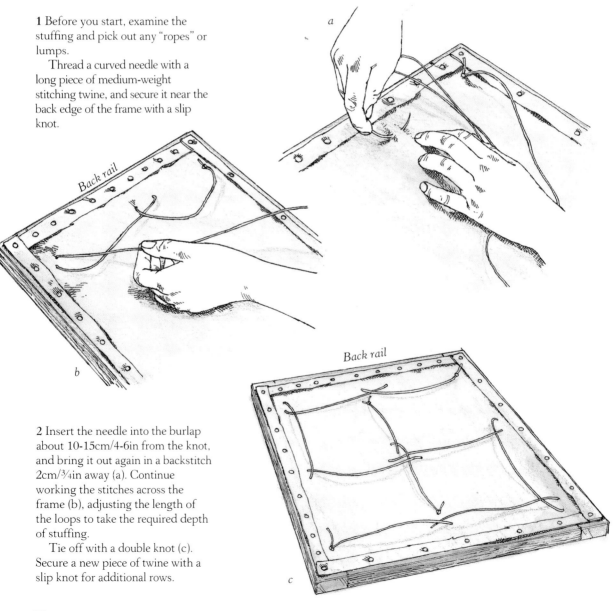

2 Insert the needle into the burlap about 10-15cm/4-6in from the knot, and bring it out again in a backstitch 2cm/¾in away (a). Continue working the stitches across the frame (b), adjusting the length of the loops to take the required depth of stuffing.

Tie off with a double knot (c). Secure a new piece of twine with a slip knot for additional rows.

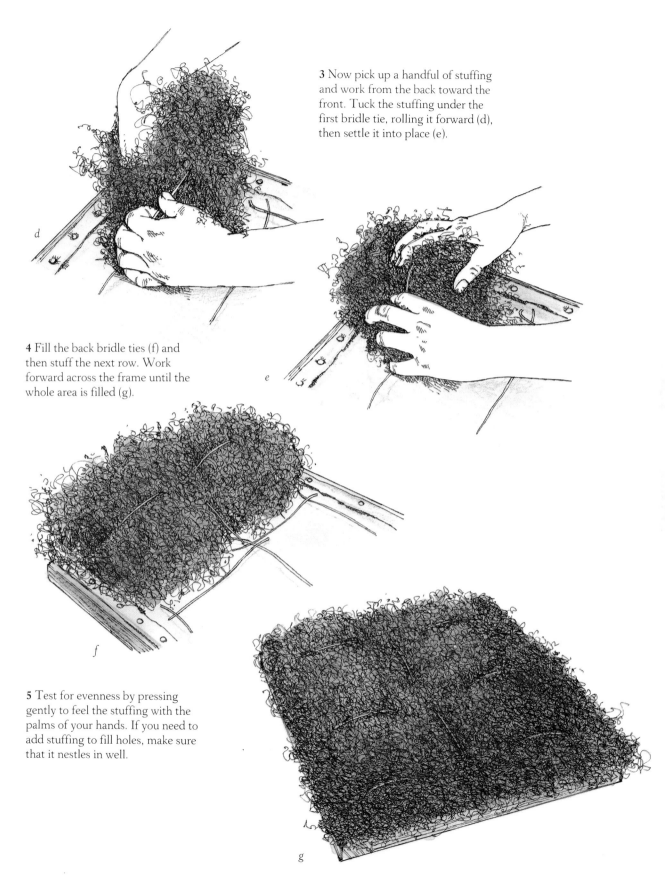

3 Now pick up a handful of stuffing and work from the back toward the front. Tuck the stuffing under the first bridle tie, rolling it forward (d), then settle it into place (e).

d

e

4 Fill the back bridle ties (f) and then stuff the next row. Work forward across the frame until the whole area is filled (g).

f

5 Test for evenness by pressing gently to feel the stuffing with the palms of your hands. If you need to add stuffing to fill holes, make sure that it nestles in well.

g

Pin-stuffed Pad

The thinnest and simplest of all the upholstery pads, pin (or pincushion) stuffing is deceptive in its simplicity. It must be worked with great care and precision, since the slightest mistakes will show. At all stages of working make sure that the materials, particularly the webbing, do not form unsightly lumpy edges, and keep the weave of the muslin square to the frame. Materials are commonly tacked off to the top of the frame as shown here, and bridle ties should be well within the frame to give a shallow edge. The pad can be stuffed with hair or polished black fiber (shown here), or with layers of batting. In the leather-covered dining chair project (p126) felted cotton is used in a wrap-around fashion for the inside and outside back.

The flattish, delicate line that is created by pin stuffing is used for scroll arms, slender backs, and wings, and is often seen on English Regency and turn-of-the-century furniture that has grooved show wood (remember to use small tacks when working on thin rails). It is also a suitable technique for the backs of chairs and sofas that have squabs for additional comfort, or for seats fitted with mattresses.

MATERIALS
Webbing
Burlap
Muslin
Stuffing or padding
Tacks

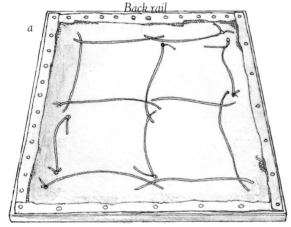

Back rail

a

Front rail

1 Fix the **webbing** (p72) and **base burlap** (p74) to the frame.

2 Sew the **bridle ties** (p76) in an appropriate arrangement for the frame, allowing for about a thumb's depth of stuffing (a). Insert the ties at the edges about 5cm/2in from the rails in order to create the characteristic slender shape.

3 Stuff into the bridle ties, creating a gentle depth at the center and thinning down to nothing at the edges (b).

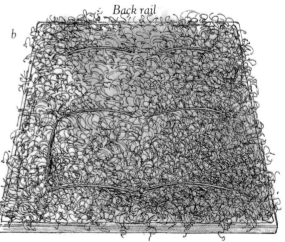

b

Back rail

Front rail

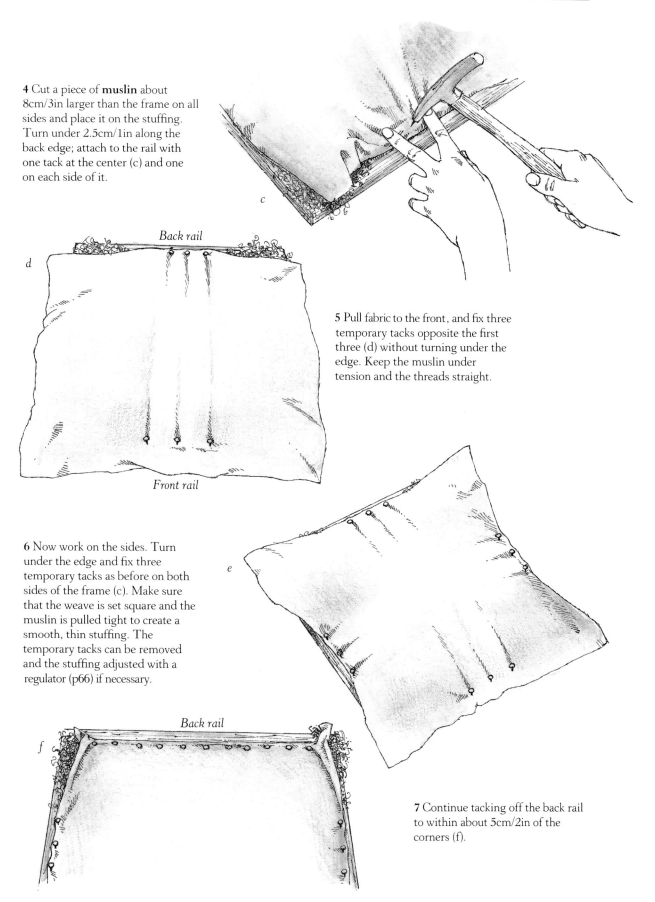

4 Cut a piece of **muslin** about 8cm/3in larger than the frame on all sides and place it on the stuffing. Turn under 2.5cm/1in along the back edge; attach to the rail with one tack at the center (c) and one on each side of it.

c

Back rail

d

Front rail

5 Pull fabric to the front, and fix three temporary tacks opposite the first three (d) without turning under the edge. Keep the muslin under tension and the threads straight.

6 Now work on the sides. Turn under the edge and fix three temporary tacks as before on both sides of the frame (c). Make sure that the weave is set square and the muslin is pulled tight to create a smooth, thin stuffing. The temporary tacks can be removed and the stuffing adjusted with a regulator (p66) if necessary.

e

Back rail

f

7 Continue tacking off the back rail to within about 5cm/2in of the corners (f).

Back rail

g

Front rail

8 Pull the muslin over to the front and continue temporary tacking, leaving the corners.

Temporary tack the side rails, leaving the corners (g).

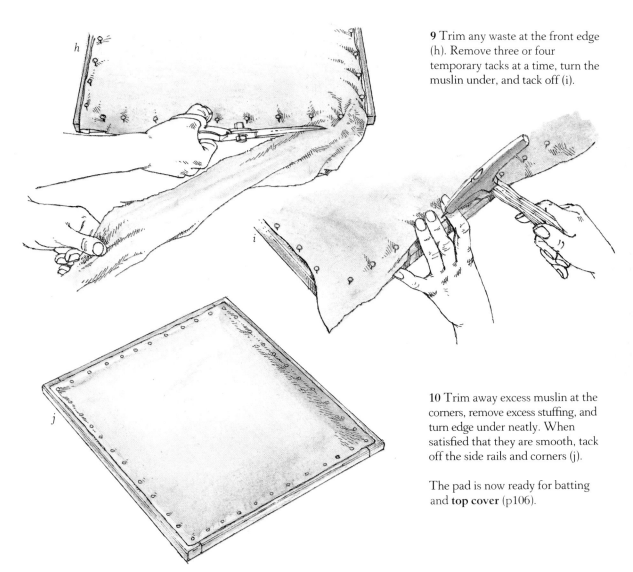

h

i

j

9 Trim any waste at the front edge (h). Remove three or four temporary tacks at a time, turn the muslin under, and tack off (i).

10 Trim away excess muslin at the corners, remove excess stuffing, and turn edge under neatly. When satisfied that they are smooth, tack off the side rails and corners (j).

The pad is now ready for batting and **top cover** (p106).

Stuffed Pad with Finger-roll Edge

The simple stuffed pad, used typically for slip seats (p116), is of basic construction, with just one stuffing into the bridle ties, which is held in place by muslin, resulting in a rounded profile. The finger-roll or thumb-roll edge gives a slightly squared, deeper, and firmer edge to stuffed pads up to about 2.5cm/1in in depth. It is constructed by stitching a border of scrim to the base burlap, stuffing, and then tacking to the front edge of the rail or to the chamfered edge (shown below right). Finger-roll edges are frequently used for wings of armchairs and the edges of slim inside-backs and arms of chairs and sofas.

The edge roll can be worked higher and wider to form a really deep and firm edge for much deeper central stuffing (which, incidentally, reflects the changes in upholstery techniques in the 17th century that evolved through the development of this roll, p23). However, a thick upholstery pad constructed with a deep edge roll will not withstand such heavy wear as a double-stuffed pad with a stitched edge (p85) and should be used only for inside backs and arms and other areas that receive less wear (see iron-framed armchair project, p138).

A quicker method of achieving a similar effect can be obtained through the tack roll. If the frame is wide enough, the strip of scrim can be tacked off through the base burlap onto the frame instead of being stitched. However, although it takes longer, I prefer stitching, because it creates a smoother roll and simply produces better work.

The instructions that follow are for building a finger-roll edge on the front of a pad to create a depth of about 2.5cm/1in.

MATERIALS
Webbing
Burlap
Scrim
Tacks
Twine
Stuffing
Muslin

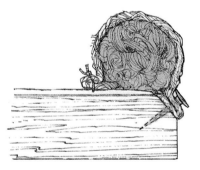

1 Attach the **webbing** (p72) and the **base burlap** (p74) to the frame.

2 Cut a piece of scrim for the **edge roll** about 12cm/5in wide by the length required plus an extra 10-12cm/4-5in; thread a curved needle with twine. Fold under 3cm/1¼in of the scrim, and place the folded edge about 4cm/1½in back from the edge of the front rail.

Secure the twine with a slip knot or a tack hold (p68), and backstitch (a) neatly along the edge of the fold, securing the scrim to the base burlap.

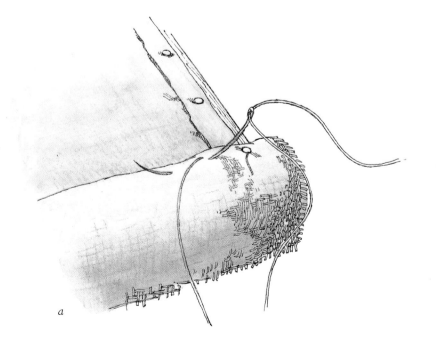

a

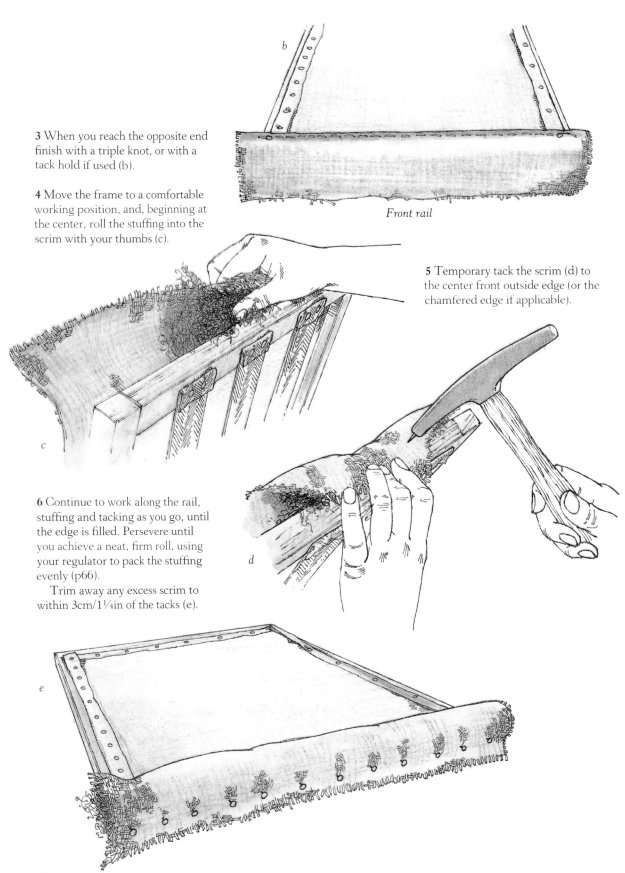

3 When you reach the opposite end finish with a triple knot, or with a tack hold if used (b).

4 Move the frame to a comfortable working position, and, beginning at the center, roll the stuffing into the scrim with your thumbs (c).

Front rail

5 Temporary tack the scrim (d) to the center front outside edge (or the chamfered edge if applicable).

6 Continue to work along the rail, stuffing and tacking as you go, until the edge is filled. Persevere until you achieve a neat, firm roll, using your regulator to pack the stuffing evenly (p66).

Trim away any excess scrim to within 3cm/1¼in of the tacks (e).

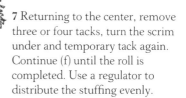

7 Returning to the center, remove three or four tacks, turn the scrim under and temporary tack again. Continue (f) until the roll is completed. Use a regulator to distribute the stuffing evenly.

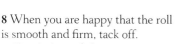

8 When you are happy that the roll is smooth and firm, tack off.
  Finish the ends by turning under and tacking off neatly on the side rails (g).

9 If you are working edge rolls on the sides as well, the stuffing of the second roll will butt firmly and neatly up to the first, and the scrim will overlap at the corner (h).

Second edge roll   First edge roll

h

10 Stitch the **bridle ties** into the base burlap and **stuff** into the bridle ties up to, but not over, the edge roll (i), making sure that the stuffing is firmly compacted at this point; anything less will flatten in use, leaving the edge in ugly relief.

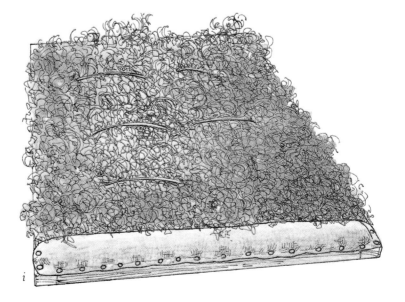

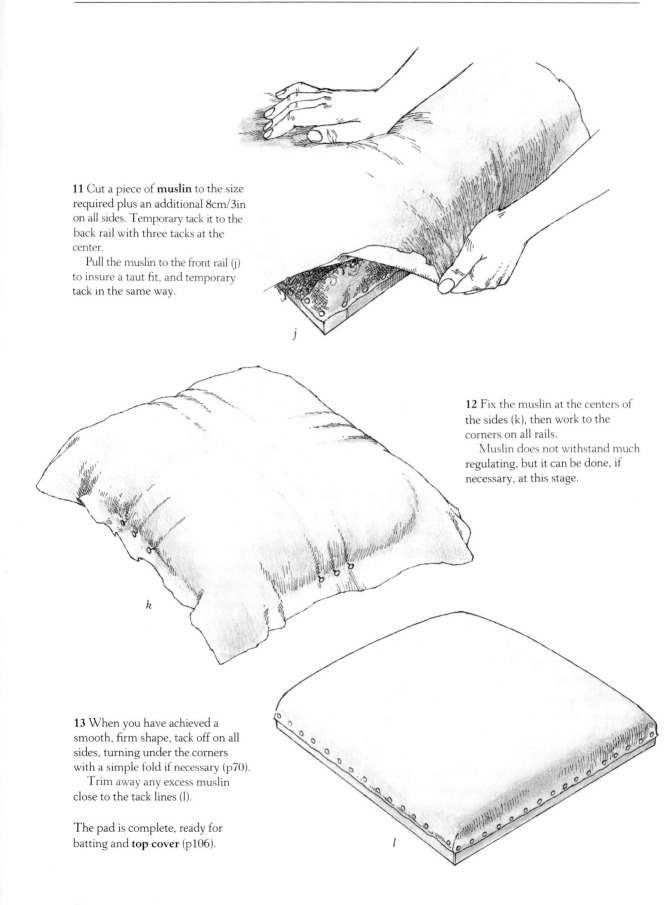

11 Cut a piece of **muslin** to the size required plus an additional 8cm/3in on all sides. Temporary tack it to the back rail with three tacks at the center.

Pull the muslin to the front rail (j) to insure a taut fit, and temporary tack in the same way.

j

12 Fix the muslin at the centers of the sides (k), then work to the corners on all rails.

Muslin does not withstand much regulating, but it can be done, if necessary, at this stage.

k

13 When you have achieved a smooth, firm shape, tack off on all sides, turning under the corners with a simple fold if necessary (p70).

Trim away any excess muslin close to the tack lines (l).

The pad is complete, ready for batting and **top cover** (p106).

l

Double-stuffed Stitched Pad

This durable pad with its firm edges forms the basis of all substantial upholstery and can be created to almost any depth from about 2.5cm/1in. The pad is stuffed twice: the first stuffing is covered with scrim and pulled flat with stuffing ties: then a second (or top) stuffing of hair or fiber into bridle ties, or a filling of felted cotton and polyester batting (without bridle ties), is added to soften the shape, which may be almost flat or roundly domed.

The walls of the pad are built up with neatly spaced rows of stitches that pack the stuffing tightly against the scrim cover to create a flat, firm border. Regulating the stuffing and the position of the stitches determines the shape of the wall. Edges may be sharply square (even right-angled if defined by close blanket stitches along the extreme edge) or softly rolled. The pad can be sculpted to overhang the frame (see p161, the arm of the chesterfield project), or set well back from the edge of the frame for a crisp, square edge (see p132, inside back of the late Victorian armchair project).

The double-stuffed stitched pad is used for dining chairs, heavy-duty seats, inside backs, arms, and some wings of chairs and sofas.

The instructions that follow create a pad about 6cm/2½in deep at the edges. The number of rows of blind and top stitches should be adjusted to suit pads of other depths.

MATERIALS
Webbing
Burlap
Tacks and twine
Stuffing
Scrim
Muslin

1 Attach the **webbing** (p72) and **base burlap** (p74) to the frame. Insert the **bridle ties** (p76). Stuff evenly with particular firmness and fullness on the edge to be stitched.

2 Cut a piece of **scrim** to cover the whole area of the stuffing, plus an additional 8cm/3in on all sides. Place on the stuffing with the weave square to the frame.

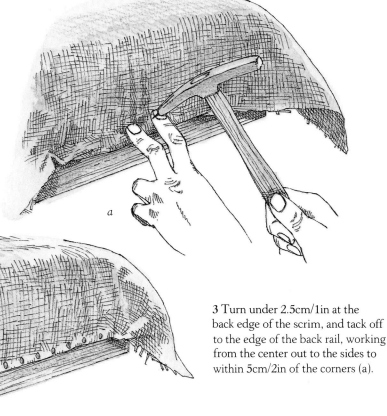

a

3 Turn under 2.5cm/1in at the back edge of the scrim, and tack off to the edge of the back rail, working from the center out to the sides to within 5cm/2in of the corners (a).

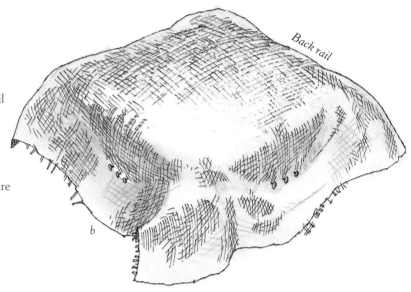

Back rail

4 Pull the scrim over to the front rail keeping the threads square. Fix three temporary tacks at the center front.

Temporary tack at the center of the side rails in the same way (b), making sure that the scrim is set square and compressing the stuffing to the required thickness, giving the correct height at the edges.

b

c

5 On the front rail continue to temporary tack to within 5cm/2in of the corners. Work the side edges in the same way (c).

If you are working on a frame with upright rails, the corners should be cut and fitted at this stage (p124).

6 Trim away excess scrim to within 2.5cm/1in of the tack line at the front and sides (d).

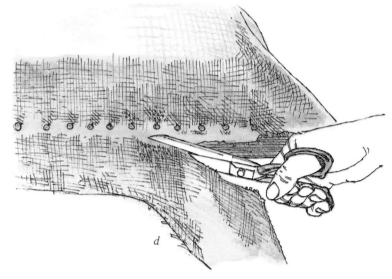

d

7 Make sure that the walls are firmly packed: remove the temporary tacks a few at a time and adjust the stuffing, adding or removing as necessary (e). Replace the temporary tacks as you go.

8 Now, starting at the center of the front edge, again remove a few temporary tacks at a time, turn the scrim under, and temporary tack it to the rail (f).

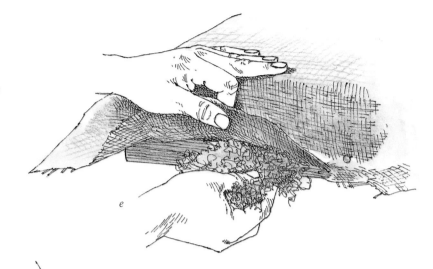

e

f

9 Work along the edge, leaving the corners free and keeping the scrim taut and straight. Work the side edges in the same way (g).

10 Fold and tack the corners (p70), keeping the edges of the pad straight and level. When satisfied that the pad is a good shape, and that the scrim is taut but not dragging the stuffing out of shape, tack off all around.

g

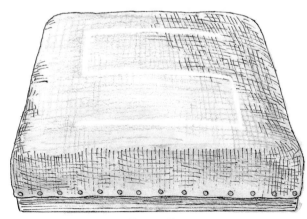

h

Front rail

11 The **stuffing ties** can now be inserted. These are long running stitches (about 10-12cm/4-5in at 2.5cm/1in intervals) made through the whole of the pad. Plan the stitches (mark them with chalk if you like) to cover the pad, following the pattern shown (h), to within about 9cm/3½in of the side edges.

12 Thread a 25cm/10in double-pointed straight needle (p54) with a generous length of stitching twine. Work from the back of the frame, inserting the needle right through the pad and bringing it back up close by. Secure with a slip knot (i).

Back rail

i

13 Work across the pad (j), gently pulling up the twine to keep the ties firm. Make sure that the bottom stitch takes up about 2.5cm/1in of the burlap and/or webbing so that it will withstand the strain when the ties are pulled tight.

j

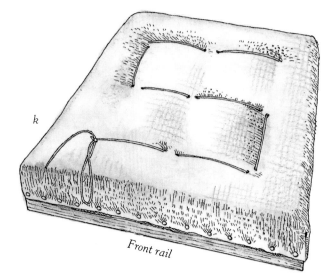

k

Front rail

14 Secure with a temporary bow which can be quickly released when the ties are pulled tight (k).

If you are working this pad on a sprung base, avoid looping the twine around the lower coils of the springs. Stitch only to the base burlap and to the top of any coils where stitched to the burlap.

15 Before making the edge stitching, regulate the edges of the pad again, pulling the stuffing forward so it overhangs the rail slightly (l); it will be pulled back to align with the rail when the stitches are locked tight and compress the stuffing. Regulate to the required height.

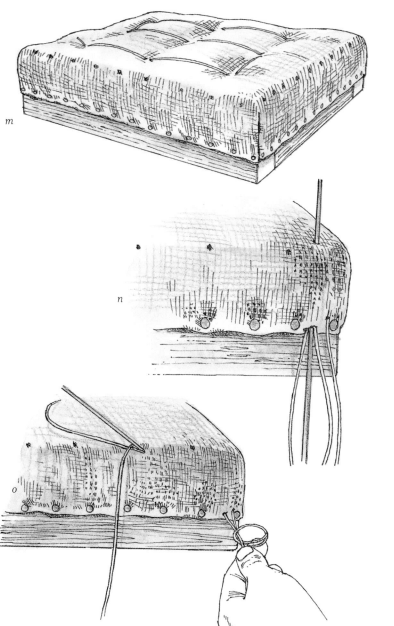

16 Regulate the stuffing along the line that will be the top edge of the wall. The holes that remain will provide a guide for the final row of top stitches (m). You might find it useful to mark the line with chalk.

17 Now make the locked blind **edge stitches**, which loop twine around the stuffing and pull it forward. Thread a 25cm/10in double-pointed straight needle with a long piece of stitching twine, and fasten it onto the pad as follows.

Insert the unthreaded end of the needle into the scrim at one side of the frame immediately above the tack rail. Angle the needle so that it pierces the scrim no more than 8cm/3in away from the edge to avoid the stuffing ties. Pull the needle through until the eye is just below the surface of the scrim; then scoop the eye end around the stuffing and return the needle back to the frame edge, piercing the scrim 1cm/½in from the point of insertion (n). Pull the needle through and push it into the pad (using it as a pincushion), leaving both hands free to fasten the twine with a slip knot (o).

18 Now work a row of locked blind stitches. Insert the needle 4cm/ 1½in from the slip knot. Pierce the top of the stuffing as before, scooping the needle to return it halfway between the point of insertion of this stitch and the slip knot (p).

19 Push through about three-quarters of the needle's length, and loop the twine that leads from the previous stitch around the needle three times (q).

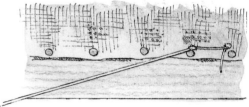

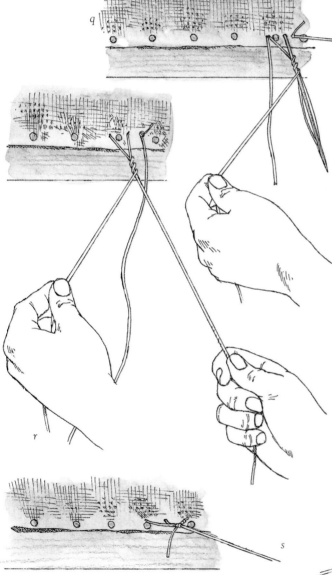

20 Remove the needle, pulling it through the looped twines, and place it in the pad. Lock the stitch (r), maintaining an even tension. To get the feel of the loop tugging at the stuffing, rest your fingers on the loop as you pull the twine through with your other hand, and, as you close the loop, pull firmly to compress the stuffing hard against the scrim. Pull the twine backward to close the winding twines and forward to lock the stitch tight (s). Do not pull too tight – this will drag the stuffing back from the edge of the frame.

Continue along the edge and fasten off by winding both twines around the needle three times.

If you run out of twine fasten off and start the new twine with a slip knot. Tidy up ends by pushing them into the pad with the needle.

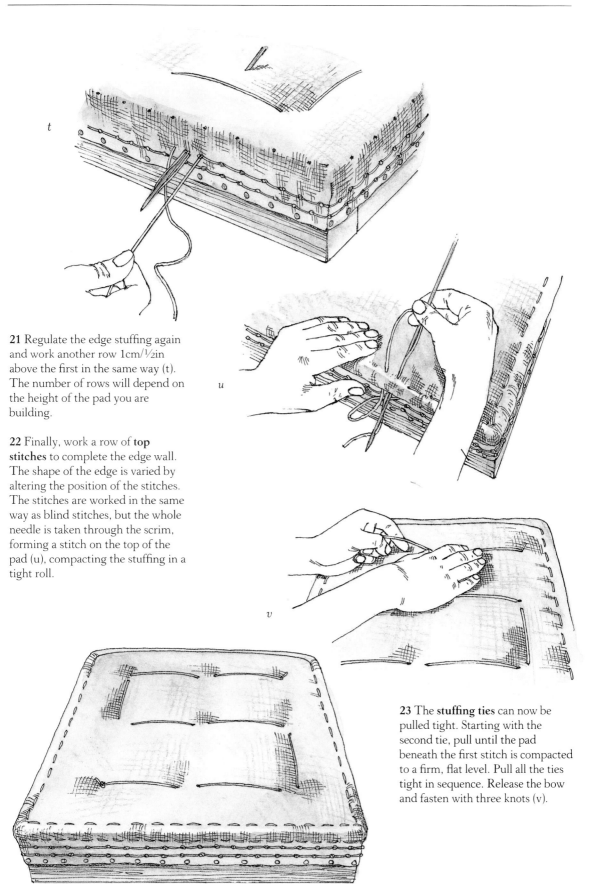

21 Regulate the edge stuffing again and work another row 1cm/½in above the first in the same way (t). The number of rows will depend on the height of the pad you are building.

22 Finally, work a row of **top stitches** to complete the edge wall. The shape of the edge is varied by altering the position of the stitches. The stitches are worked in the same way as blind stitches, but the whole needle is taken through the scrim, forming a stitch on the top of the pad (u), compacting the stuffing in a tight roll.

23 The **stuffing ties** can now be pulled tight. Starting with the second tie, pull until the pad beneath the first stitch is compacted to a firm, flat level. Pull all the ties tight in sequence. Release the bow and fasten with three knots (v).

24 Insert **bridle ties** into the pad with fairly small loops to allow for a light second (top) stuffing (w). (No bridle ties are used for felted cotton filling.)

25 Stuff into the bridle ties, molding to the required shape and degree of comfort (x).

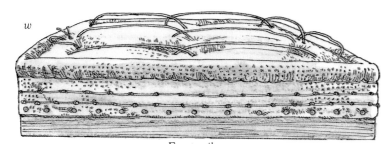

Front rail

26 Cut a piece of **muslin** 8cm/3in larger overall than the area to be covered. Temporary tack along the back rail (without turning under the edge) to within 5cm/2in of the corners. Pull over to the front rail, compressing the top stuffing, and fix three temporary tacks at the center. Fix three temporary tacks at the sides, making sure that the muslin is set square and that the top stuffing creates a good line (y).

Cut and fit the corners of upright back rails at this stage.

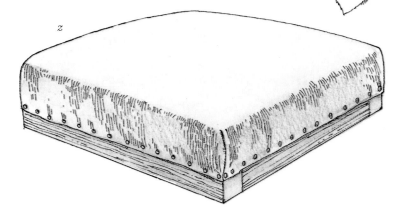

27 Temporary tack the front edge to within 5cm/2in of the corners, then work on the sides in the same way. Fold and finish all corners.

When you are satisfied with the finish, hammer home all the tacks and trim away excess muslin to the tack line (z).

The pad is complete, ready for batting and **top cover** (p106).

Springing

Springs are really a filling sandwiched between the webbing and the base burlap (or spring canvas) which add resilience, depth, comfort, and durability to seats and inside backs, as well as to the tops of armpads and inside arms of large chairs and sofas. Springs may also be used to create shape – for example, by using higher springs in the center of a seat.

The springs are fastened in place by being stitched to the webbing below, lashed together and to the frame, and then stitched to the burlap above. They are thus totally secured to both the frame and the upholstery pad. There are two cardinal rules: first, springs of the correct size and gauge must be used (p54); second, they should be lashed so that they compress vertically when in use. If they list to one side, they will distort in use and be uncomfortable, eventually destroying the upholstery.

The frame and the shape of the pad determine the pattern of the springs. Lashing ties are generally secured in straight lines, from one side of the rail to the other (see below). A typical plan for a substantial seat would be three rows of three springs, or one row of three and two rows of four.

The stuffed pad is worked over the spring canvas. This may be a simple stuffed pad, or, more commonly, a double-stuffed stitched pad, as in the seats of the late Victorian armchair (p132) and the *chaise longue* (p146) and the back and arms of the chesterfield (p160), or a deck, as in the wing chair (p152) and the chesterfield (p160).

A sprung edge can be worked on the front rail of a seat for additional comfort (p154). This row of springs is worked independently of the main body of springs and is secured at the front with twine to an edge wire (p97).

MATERIALS
Webbing
Tacks
Chalk
Spring needle
Stitching twine
Double-cone springs
Laid cord
Heavyweight burlap

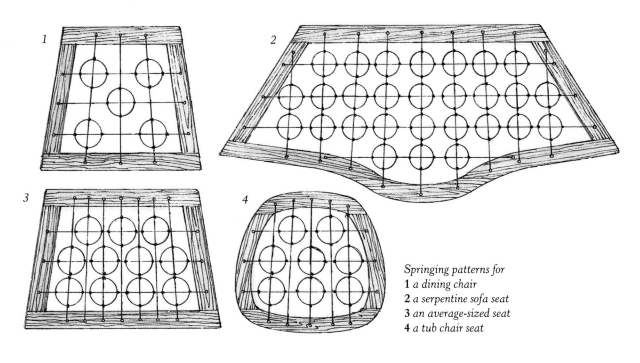

Springing patterns for
1 *a dining chair*
2 *a serpentine sofa seat*
3 *an average-sized seat*
4 *a tub chair seat*

1 Fix the **webbing** to the underside (or outside) of the rail, rather than on the top or inside of rails, as for unsprung pads. Place the webs close enough together to support the base of the springs.

2 Plan the pattern of the springs on the webs. The springs should be evenly distributed over the whole area within the frame (p93), but they should not touch each other when compressed or be too close to the edges of the frame. On seats, place springs near the front rail for firmness where the seat receives most wear; leave space at the back to allow for the swell of the inside back stuffing.

On this seat frame, which tapers slightly at the back, three rows of springs are required: three springs in the back row and two rows of four springs.

You may find it helpful to mark spring positions with chalk.

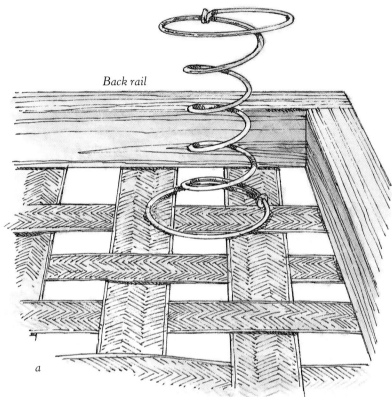

Back rail

a

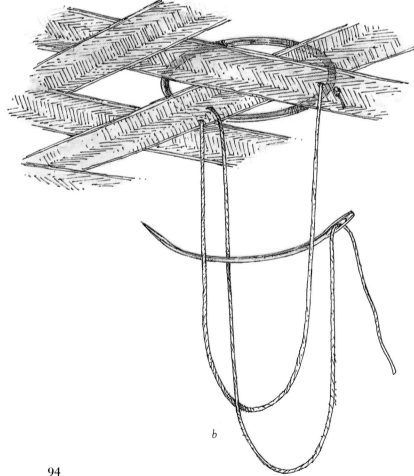

b

3 Stitch the base of each spring to the webbing at three equidistant points to ensure stability.

Thread a spring needle with a long length of stitching twine or nylon twine. Start with the spring at the back right-hand corner of the frame; position it so that the metal knuckle on the base coil is supported by webbing (a).

4 Insert the needle from underneath the web, bringing it up close to the spring. Loop the twine over the bottom coil and fasten with a slip knot (p68) underneath. Take the needle across to the second point and, leaving a large loop of twine hanging below the webbing, bring it up through to the top and over the coil as before. Take the needle back down through the webbing so that the twine hangs down, then scoop the needle straight through the loop (b). Pull smoothly back in the direction of the previous stitch, then tighten off with a sharp pull forward. Make the third spring tie.

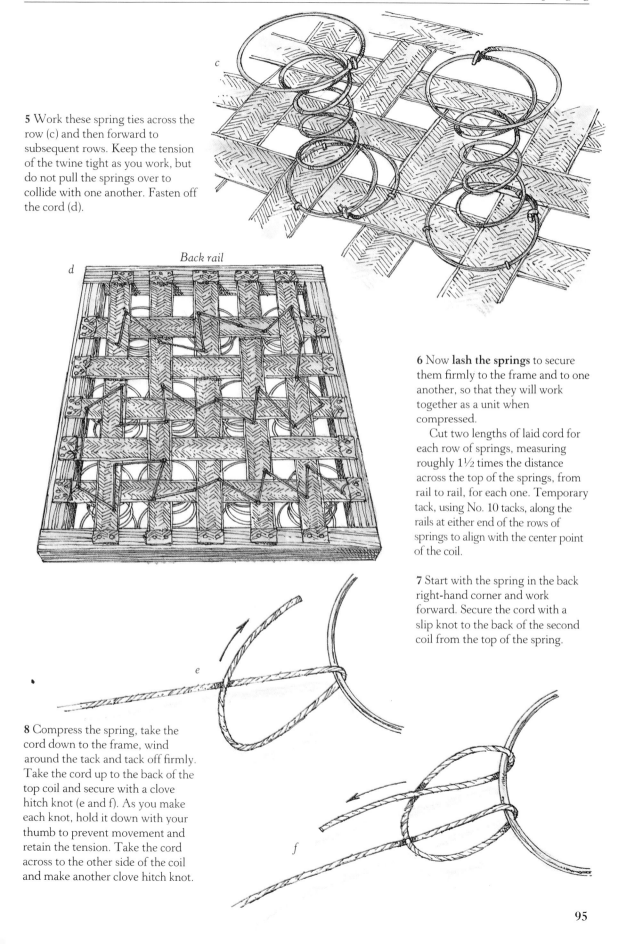

c

5 Work these spring ties across the row (c) and then forward to subsequent rows. Keep the tension of the twine tight as you work, but do not pull the springs over to collide with one another. Fasten off the cord (d).

Back rail

d

6 Now **lash the springs** to secure them firmly to the frame and to one another, so that they will work together as a unit when compressed.

Cut two lengths of laid cord for each row of springs, measuring roughly 1½ times the distance across the top of the springs, from rail to rail, for each one. Temporary tack, using No. 10 tacks, along the rails at either end of the rows of springs to align with the center point of the coil.

7 Start with the spring in the back right-hand corner and work forward. Secure the cord with a slip knot to the back of the second coil from the top of the spring.

e

8 Compress the spring, take the cord down to the frame, wind around the tack and tack off firmly. Take the cord up to the back of the top coil and secure with a clove hitch knot (e and f). As you make each knot, hold it down with your thumb to prevent movement and retain the tension. Take the cord across to the other side of the coil and make another clove hitch knot.

f

95

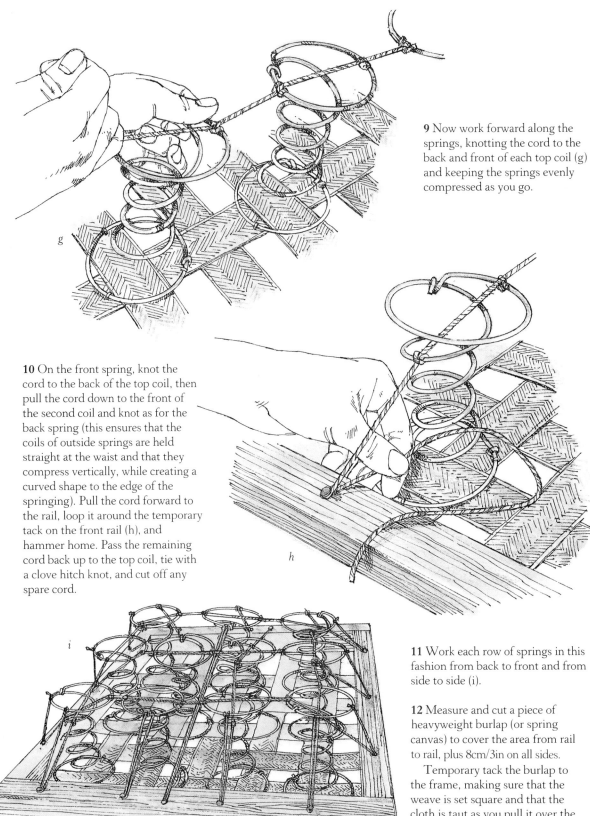

9 Now work forward along the springs, knotting the cord to the back and front of each top coil (g) and keeping the springs evenly compressed as you go.

10 On the front spring, knot the cord to the back of the top coil, then pull the cord down to the front of the second coil and knot as for the back spring (this ensures that the coils of outside springs are held straight at the waist and that they compress vertically, while creating a curved shape to the edge of the springing). Pull the cord forward to the rail, loop it around the temporary tack on the front rail (h), and hammer home. Pass the remaining cord back up to the top coil, tie with a clove hitch knot, and cut off any spare cord.

11 Work each row of springs in this fashion from back to front and from side to side (i).

12 Measure and cut a piece of heavyweight burlap (or spring canvas) to cover the area from rail to rail, plus 8cm/3in on all sides.

Temporary tack the burlap to the frame, making sure that the weave is set square and that the cloth is taut as you pull it over the springs. Tack home to give a firm tension.

Front rail

13 Stitch the top of the springs to the burlap. Starting with a slip knot, stitch each spring at three equidistant points on the top coil using spring ties, in the same way as securing the base of the springs to the webbing (j).

14 The sprung base is now complete and ready for a stuffed pad to be worked onto it (k).

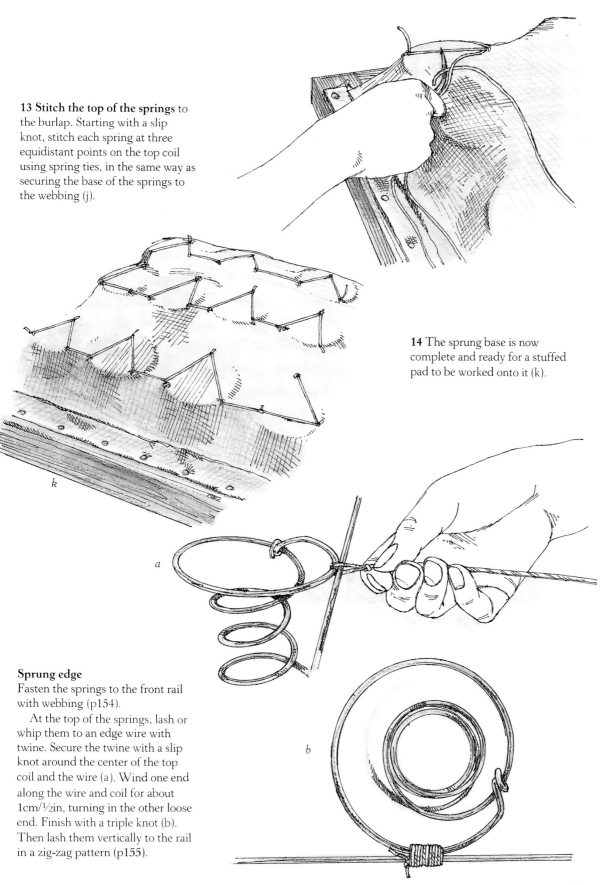

Sprung edge
Fasten the springs to the front rail with webbing (p154).

At the top of the springs, lash or whip them to an edge wire with twine. Secure the twine with a slip knot around the center of the top coil and the wire (a). Wind one end along the wire and coil for about 1cm/½in, turning in the other loose end. Finish with a triple knot (b). Then lash them vertically to the rail in a zig-zag pattern (p155).

Pleated tufting

The secret of pleated tufting, given that your technique is sound, is your creative input, and this is what makes it so satisfying. There is no need to be apprehensive about tufting. Make sure that all your materials are set square and take accurate measurements. Pay careful attention to fixing the muslin as preparation for giving a really good finish to the top cover. If you work each stage calmly and thoroughly, you will enjoy the visual and sensuous drama created by the smooth swells and deep valleys, defined by precise folds and accentuated by tiny buttons at the final stage when you fit the top cover.

The pleated tufting method I use is created on a double-stuffed stitched pad (p85), worked to the stitched scrim stage. The depth of the first stuffing and the subsequent top filling of felted cotton and polyester batting should be adjusted to a depth to suit the frame and the arrangement of the tufting. If I wish to smother a small area with a tiny tufting pattern of relatively shallow depth, I create a base pad about 2.5cm/1in deep, whereas for deeper, more widely spaced tufting I use a base pad 5-8cm/2-3in deep.

I always do the tufting by eye, which allows me the freedom to explore circular and unusually arranged patterns, but you should first master the conventional pattern, which I demonstrate here, in which the length of the tufted diamond is greater than the width.

Pleated tufting can be used for inside backs, seats, arms, padded borders, rails, and, for a really extravagant effect, on outside arms and backs. In fact, it can be used on all types of furniture whose frames allow for a pad deep enough to accommodate the tufting and which will be aesthetically enhanced by this treatment.

MATERIALS
Webbing
Base burlap
Twine
Stuffing
Scrim
Felted cotton
Polyester batting
Muslin

1 Work a **double-stuffed stitched pad** (p85, up to step 22, fig. u) to the depth you require (for this square frame I have worked it 5cm/2in high at the edge of the wall). You do not need to insert stuffing ties, since the tufting will hold everything firm. However, you may prefer to do so, since they will keep materials square and under control as you work.

2 Mark the **tufting pattern** by eye, pushing large tacks or skewers into the pad.

The pattern should be balanced within the frame, allowing for generous space at the edges. As a general rule, the depth of the diamond shape created should be longer than it is wide. The pattern shown for a square frame will give you a starting point, but you should respond to the shape of the chair.

On the inside backs of many armchairs it is best to site the bottom row of buttons just above the small of the back, creating a lumbar area.

When you are happy with the arrangement, adjust the tacks to space them out accurately. Measure with a flexible tape and mark the button positions on the outside edges of the pad. Draw diagonal chalk or pen lines on the pad as shown to find the position of central buttons. Double-check the measurements.

On long frames, work tufting patterns in 60cm/24in panels.

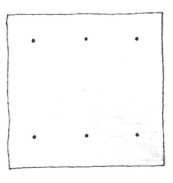

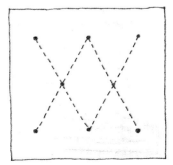

3 Make a cross **cut into the scrim** with scissors centered on a button point. Cut into the stuffing, working a hole with your finger until you can reach the base burlap (a). Repeat at each button point (b).

a

b

4 Pull off two pieces of **felted cotton** large enough to cover the top and sides of the pad. Place both layers on the scrim and pull out holes with your fingers (c).

5 Cut a piece of polyester batting about 20cm/8in larger overall than the pad. Place it on the felted cotton and cut out holes that correspond with the holes in the cotton (d).

c

d

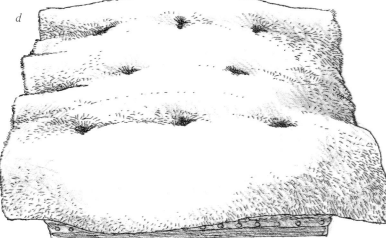

6 Measure for the **muslin**: run a tape measure over the pad from rail to rail in both directions at the widest point, pushing the tape down into the holes; add about 8cm/3in on all sides. Cut the muslin and fold it down the center vertically, marking the top if necessary.

7 Cut a 40cm/15in length of twine for each **button tie**, and thread a straight needle.

Start with the central hole of the back row. Push the muslin into the hole with your fingers, then insert the needle, guiding it with the index finger of your other hand (e). Take the needle through the pad, unthread the needle, and re-thread it on the twine remaining on the muslin side and push it through to the underside, taking a small stitch. Fasten with a slip knot, inserting a small rolled square of muslin into the loop (f) to prevent the twine from pulling through the burlap. The buttons will be threaded on later when the top cover is fitted.

e

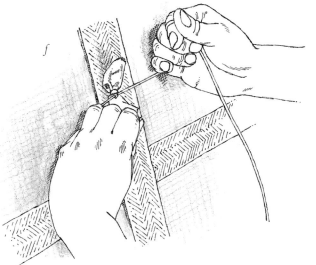

f

8 Work the remaining buttoning ties in the row on either side of the center, making sure that the muslin is stretched taut and square over the pad.

9 Move forward to a button in the next row, using the central fold as a guide and following the weave of the muslin. Push the muslin into the hole, forming diamond folds between the first row and the second. When you are happy that the muslin is square and taut, insert the ties and complete the row.

10 Work forward in this way until all the rows are completed (g).

11 Use the flat end of the regulator to neaten the button folds, smoothing down the diagonal creases between the buttons and pushing the flat end into the fold. Use a skewer to pull the fold into shape.

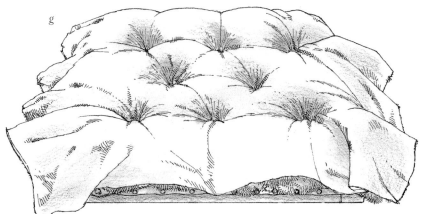

g

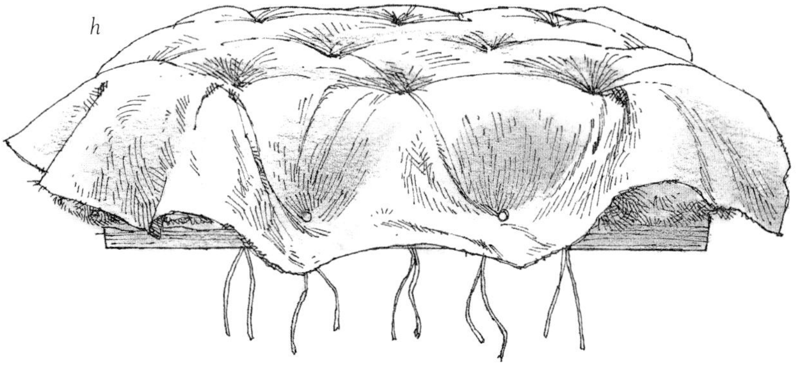

12 Now tack the muslin onto the rails. Temporary tack all around the rails at a central point between each button position (h).

13 At each edge smooth the muslin from the center toward the sides, folding the excess material to make wrinkle-free walls with neat folds running straight down from the button ties. On the side rails folds should face forward; on the front and back rails they should face the same direction (except where there is an even number, in which case they can be folded toward the center). Temporary tack the folds in position at all the button points (i).

14 When you are satisfied that the walls and folds are smooth and taut, temporary tack the spaces between the buttons, and neatly fold the corners (j).

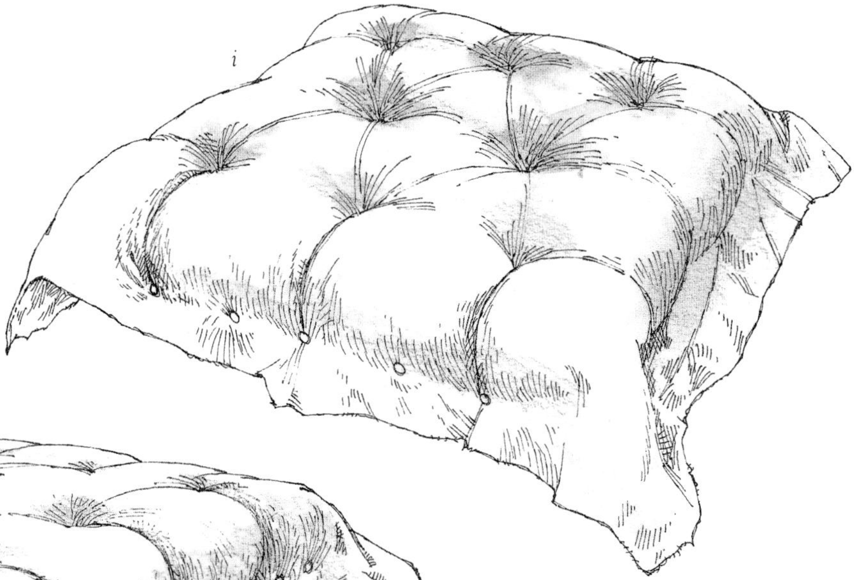

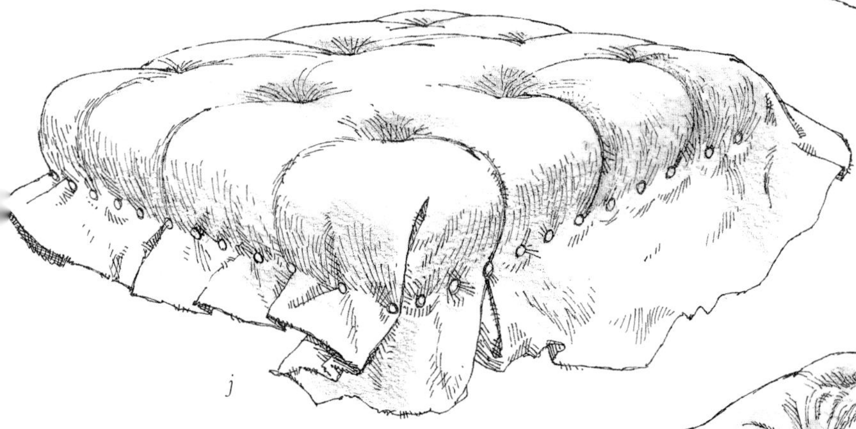

15 If the chair has upright rails the corners should be cut and fitted at this point (p122).

16 Tack off and trim the muslin to the tack line (k). Your pad is now ready for batting and **top cover** (p106). The buttons will be looped onto the twine and settled flat against the seat base.

h

i

j

k

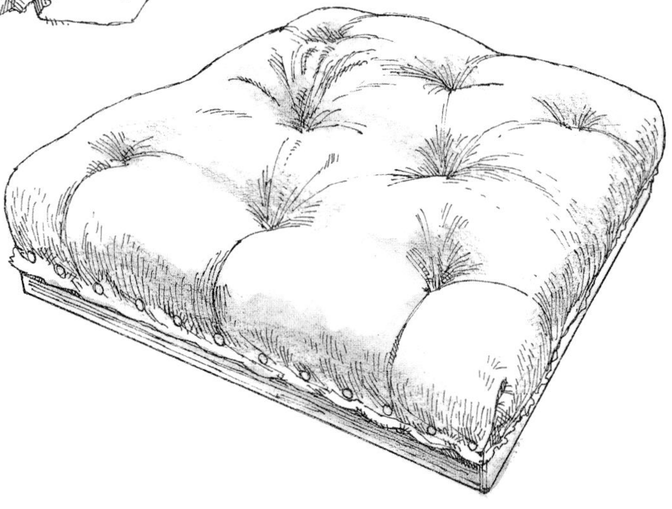

Cushions and Pillows

Many upholstered chairs and sofas incorporate boxed cushions, which are constructed with a kind of gusset, called boxing, in order to fit snugly into the seat and back. Properly made, these cushions add sumptuous ease, but if they are overstuffed or skimpy, ill-fitting, or made to the wrong depth they will spoil both appearance and comfort.

Bolsters add style to many sofas, notably chesterfields, and are frequently an integral part of the design of the frame. Traditionally made of horsehair and linen, they are today more commonly stuffed with feathers.

Small, flat scatter pillows can be placed under the neck or in the small of the back, or used purely as decorative features. They come in many different shapes and sizes. But unless you are using fabric scraps and left-over feathers from upholstery cushions, it really is not worth the cost in time and money to make them yourself. Instead, a department store will provide most shapes and sizes at a reasonable cost.

Whatever its precise function, the primary purpose of a cushion should be to provide comfort. Feathers are the best filling unless a very firm pad is required, in which case, high density flame-retardant foam works well. If you are using feathers, choose from the following, all of which are sold by weight: chopped feathers (short and sharp, cheap and unpleasant); curled feathers (satisfying and comfortable); feather and down (producing a light, soft cushion, more expensive than curled feathers, cheaper than down – a good compromise); and down (very light, very soft, and very expensive). If you are deterred by allergies, choose a synthetic alternative to feathers.

Use waxed cambric for the inner cushion or pillow, with the shiny surface on the inside to prevent the feathers from escaping.

The amount of filling used is an important consideration. Most faulty cushions suffer from over-stuffing. The feathers are so solidly packed that they are unable to expand, resulting in a heavy, stodgy effect. Understuffing is equally unsatisfactory, however, so be prepared to experiment before machine stitching the final seam.

Boxed cushion

It is important to give as much thought and care to making a boxed cushion as to the seat on which it will rest. A well-cut template will ensure the correct fit and depth of the cushion. When making the template, remember that boxed cushions should be made 1cm/½in larger on all sides than the seat so that the feathers spread out comfortably inside the top cover. Bear in mind the finished height of the deck if you are measuring the depth of the boxing before completing the rest of the upholstery. The cushion will compress to about half its height when sat upon.

Unless small, these cushions should have internal walls so that channeled sections are created. This prevents feathers from gathering at the sides leaving the center bald and hard.

The instructions that follow show how to make a cushion incorporating two internal walls. It is shaped at the front to fit around the arms of a chair.

MATERIALS
Waxed cambric
Paper for template
Filling (e.g. feathers)
Strong sewing thread

Boxed cushion

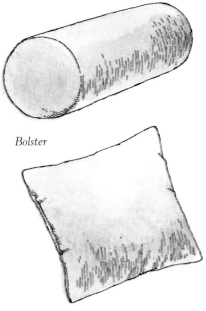

Bolster

Scatter pillow

1 Make the template. Take a large sheet of paper (sturdy brown wrapping paper is best), and cut it roughly to shape (larger than needed). Place the paper on the seat, folding the edges until an exact fit is achieved. Remember to allow for the swell of the arm and the inside back upholstery within the depth of the cushion. Remove the paper, fold it lengthwise down the center and trim it to the folds, so that the shape is symmetrical.

Keep this template for the top cover (p180), when you will add a seam allowance of 2cm/¾in on all sides.

2 Use the template to cut out two pieces of waxed cambric for the top and bottom of the cushion. Remember to add a 2cm/¾in seam allowance all around each piece you cut out, plus another 1cm/½in on all sides, so that the cushion fits well into its outer cover. Then cut the pieces for the boxing, which will run continuously around the cushion. Since the pieces can be joined together at any point, make the most economic use of the cambric, adding an appropriate additional seam allowance.

Finally, cut the two internal walls (which run from side to side) so that they are 2.5cm/1in deeper again than the depth of the boxing to allow for a gentle doming of the cushion. So if, for example, you wished the finished cushion pad to be 10cm/4in deep, you would cut the boxing cambric 12.5cm/5in deep and the internal walls 15cm/6in deep. This will fit a finished cushion cover 8cm/3in deep.

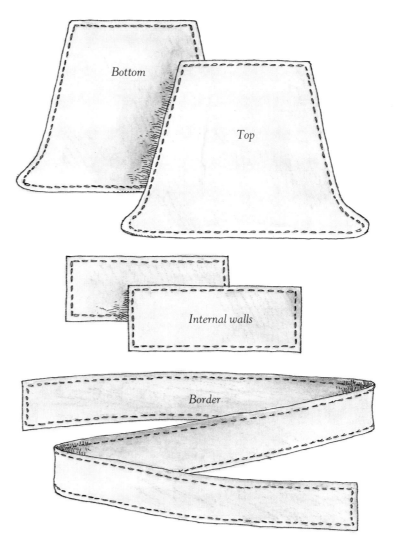

Bottom

Top

Internal walls

Border

3 Divide the surface of the cushion into thirds, side to side, and draw straight lines across the fabric on the reverse (shiny) side of both the top and bottom panels. Then sew the two internal wall sections to these guidelines, attaching one side and then the other (a).

a

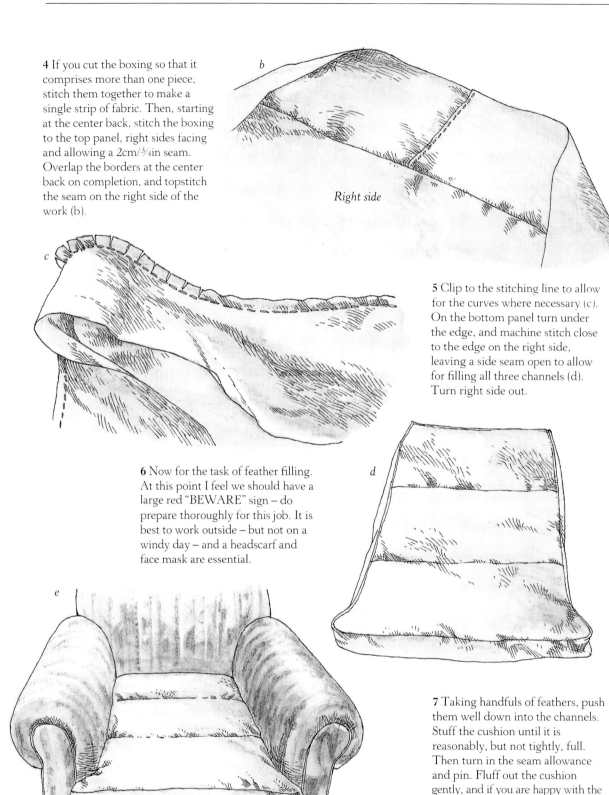

4 If you cut the boxing so that it comprises more than one piece, stitch them together to make a single strip of fabric. Then, starting at the center back, stitch the boxing to the top panel, right sides facing and allowing a 2cm/¾in seam. Overlap the borders at the center back on completion, and topstitch the seam on the right side of the work (b).

b

Right side

c

5 Clip to the stitching line to allow for the curves where necessary (c). On the bottom panel turn under the edge, and machine stitch close to the edge on the right side, leaving a side seam open to allow for filling all three channels (d). Turn right side out.

6 Now for the task of feather filling. At this point I feel we should have a large red "BEWARE" sign – do prepare thoroughly for this job. It is best to work outside – but not on a windy day – and a headscarf and face mask are essential.

d

e

7 Taking handfuls of feathers, push them well down into the channels. Stuff the cushion until it is reasonably, but not tightly, full. Then turn in the seam allowance and pin. Fluff out the cushion gently, and if you are happy with the amount of filling, compress it back into the channels and machine stitch the opening. Plump out the cushion and vacuum it to remove all the fluff. It is ready for the top cover (e and p180).

Bolster

1 Cut two end circles of the size required for the finished top cover plus 3.5cm/1¼in all the way around (for the seam and the additional allowance). Also cut one panel, the width of which should equal that of the finished length of the bolster (B) plus the statutory allowance. The depth should be that of the circumference of the end circles (A) plus a 4cm/1½in seam allowance.

2 With right sides facing, fold the main section in half lengthwise and stitch the side seam, leaving a center gap of about 15cm/6in (f). Clip the unsewn edges (A) close to the seamline to make joining easier. With right sides together, sew the end pieces in place. Clip to the seamline on the circular pieces (g).

3 Turn right side out, fill with feathers, and stitch the seam gap.

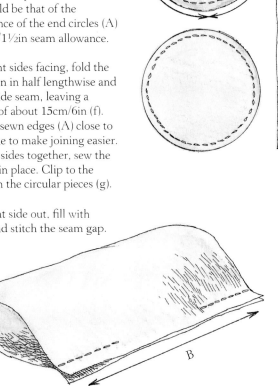

Circular ends

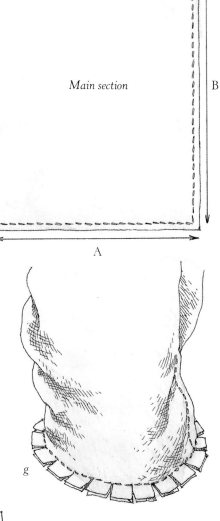

Main section

B

A

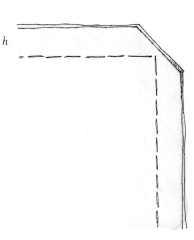

g

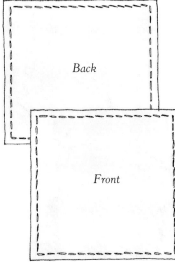

f

B

Scatter pillow

To make a scatter pillow, simply cut two pieces of cambric of the required size, with the standard seam allowance, and stitch them together, right sides facing, leaving a gap for stuffing. Clip off the corners to reduce bulk (h). Turn pillow right side out, fill with feathers, and slipstitch the gap.

Back

Front

h

Top Cover & Finishing

The top cover and trimming is, of course, the finishing touch that makes all the hard work worthwhile. But whereas icing can artfully conceal a lopsided cake, a top cover reveals, rather than disguises, lumpy lines and lean or distended shapes. So do take a critical look at the outline of your muslin work, and proceed to top cover only when you are happy with it.

Measuring for top cover

It is best to measure for top cover at muslin stage when the pad is complete. If, for practical reasons, you have to measure up when the old upholstery is still fixed to the frame, you should make an allowance for greater fullness in the finished pad. It is better not to measure up when the frame is stripped bare, because it is difficult to estimate the finished measurement. Always re-measure at muslin stage, particularly if the pad is buttoned.

Measure for all the panels of the chair cover at their deepest and widest points. As a general rule, add a 5cm/2in allowance on all sides and a 2 cm/¾in seam allowance for any panels that will be joined. The size of the pattern of the fabric will also affect the final measurement. Make a cutting list of all the pieces to be cut, always noting first the depth and then the width to prevent mistakes when planning and cutting.

Using a flexible tape measure, start with the inside back, tucking the tape right down behind the back of the seat pad to wrap around the rail to the tack-off point; run it up to the top tack rail, add the 5cm/2in allowance to both ends and make a note of the depth. Measure the width between the tack-off points on both sides and add allowances.

Measure the seat and inside arms in the same way. The outside arms, outside back, arm scrolls, wings, and front border are measured from rail to rail or from seam to rail, always at the widest point. Be generous when allowing for pieces that will fit around curves.

If you are measuring up for a buttoned or tufted pad, push the tape down into each button-tied dip, make the standard 5cm/2in allowance on all sides, and allow adequate fabric for overlapping panels when joining (p110).

Cutting plan

Use your cutting list to make a cutting plan. Draw a rectangle to represent the width of the fabric you will be using, and mark out the pieces, writing down the measurements. Work to scale on grid or graph paper if this helps. Arrange all the pieces in the most economical way, placing the largest pieces first. All the pieces should be represented by rectangles; panels should be shaped when they are fitted. If you are using piping remember to make allowance for strips cut on the bias.

Plain fabrics are the easiest to plan, but remember that even a visible directional weave creates a pattern that must be followed through from piece to piece on the chair or sofa. The direction of piled fabric, such as velvet, must run from top to bottom on backs, arms, and wings; on seats, from back to front. If the pattern repeat is obvious and needs to be matched, you will have to make allowance for this. Make sure that dominant motifs are centered, and that inside arms match each other.

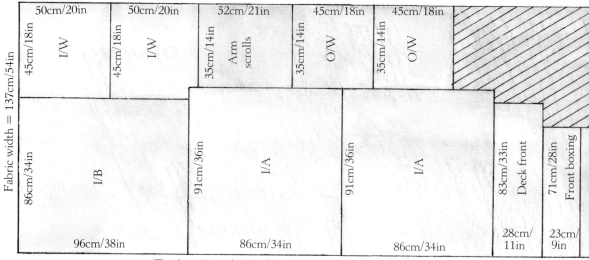

	50cm/20in		50cm/20in		52cm/21in		45cm/18in		45cm/18in	
45cm/18in	I/W	45cm/18in	I/W	35cm/14in	Arm scrolls	35cm/14in	O/W	35cm/14in	O/W	
86cm/34in	I/B		91cm/36in	I/A		91cm/36in	I/A		83cm/33in Deck front	71cm/28in Front boxing
	96cm/38in			86cm/34in			86cm/34in		28cm/11in	23cm/9in

Total = 584cm/231in. Length required = 6.5m/7yd.

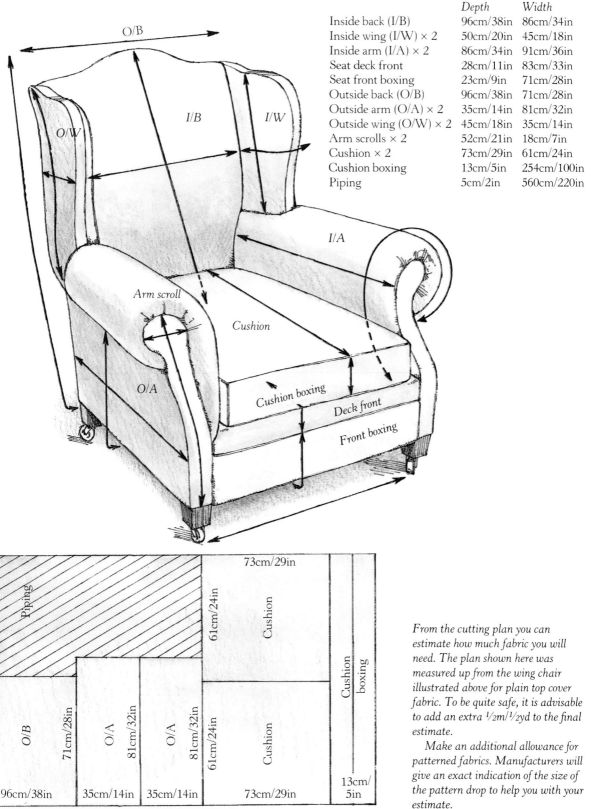

CUTTING LIST

	Depth	Width
Inside back (I/B)	96cm/38in	86cm/34in
Inside wing (I/W) × 2	50cm/20in	45cm/18in
Inside arm (I/A) × 2	86cm/34in	91cm/36in
Seat deck front	28cm/11in	83cm/33in
Seat front boxing	23cm/9in	71cm/28in
Outside back (O/B)	96cm/38in	71cm/28in
Outside arm (O/A) × 2	35cm/14in	81cm/32in
Outside wing (O/W) × 2	45cm/18in	35cm/14in
Arm scrolls × 2	52cm/21in	18cm/7in
Cushion × 2	73cm/29in	61cm/24in
Cushion boxing	13cm/5in	254cm/100in
Piping	5cm/2in	560cm/220in

From the cutting plan you can estimate how much fabric you will need. The plan shown here was measured up from the wing chair illustrated above for plain top cover fabric. To be quite safe, it is advisable to add an extra ½m/½yd to the final estimate.

Make an additional allowance for patterned fabrics. Manufacturers will give an exact indication of the size of the pattern drop to help you with your estimate.

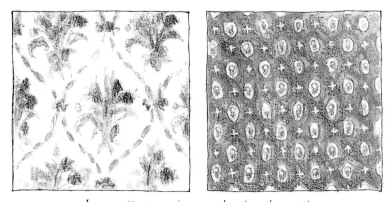

Large patterns require more planning when cutting

Marking and cutting the fabric

I recommend that you cut all the panels of fabric before you start. This is absolutely essential when working with a large pattern. If the pattern is on a relatively small scale, I sometimes cut out the pieces as I require them when fitting top cover.

You will need a large flat cutting surface (p49) or a clean floor, a straight edge, large sharp scissors or shears, tailor's chalk, and pins.

First check the fabric for flaws, then mark it out according to the cutting plan, using tailor's chalk or pins, on the right side of the fabric. Double check that the pile, weave, and/or pattern are running consistently and that motifs are correctly placed – this sounds obvious, but it is very easy to slip up, wasting time and material. Cut the fabric with care, following the weave to ensure that it is square. As soon as you have cut each piece, pin a label to the center top for identification. Store the cut pieces carefully.

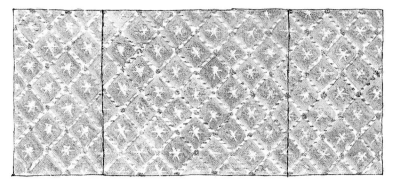

Join fabric with a large central panel

Joins and flies

If you require a piece that is larger than the full width of the fabric (for the seat or back of a sofa, for instance), you will have to join pieces with the sewing machine before they are fitted. Fabrics that are woven in unusually narrow widths, such as haircloth and some hand loomed silks, may need to be joined, even for small chairs or sofas. Joins may also have to be made in order to achieve the correct placement of a motif.

Disguise the seams as much as possible by matching the pattern carefully, and by seaming symmetrically down the sides of a piece with the large panel in the center, rather than joining in the middle.

On the other hand, you may choose to make a feature of the joins in order to re-create the appearance of pre-19th century top covering which was manufactured in 52cm/21in narrow widths (p28).

Extension flies

Joining panels of top cover on pleated tufting must be done when fitting to the pad (p110).

If you are trying to save on material or if the panels are not large enough, you can sew extension pieces, or "flies" around the sides and back of seat panels or on the bottom of inside backs and arms where they will tuck into the upholstery out of sight.

Cut flies from muslin, or other suitable material, and machine stitch them to the panel.

Batting and fitting

Before fitting the top cover on the muslin-covered pad, first cover the pad with a layer of batting. This will provide additional softness and will also prevent any hair filling from working through the muslin.

I always use polyester batting, although cotton batting does the same job. Cut the batting to fit the pad to within about 2.5cm/1in of the tack line.

Fit the inside pieces of the cover first, one at a time, in the most convenient order: usually inside back, arms, wings, seat.

Inside backs and arms can be tacked to their own bottom rails, or they can be pulled down and tacked over the seat top cover to the seat rails. The seat cover must, however, always be tacked to its own rails – never tack it to the inside back or arm rails, for it will certainly split when sat upon.

Place the top cover over the batting, checking that you are using the correct piece, the correct way up, and centering the pattern, if any, on the frame.

The top cover is fitted in the same way as muslin. Generally, you should use gimp pins or No. 3 tacks unless you are tacking through several layers of material, when a slightly longer tack should be used. Check at all times for even tension (which should be taut, but not strained), and keep the threads square to the frame.

It is particularly important to avoid "tack ties" (p67) when fitting the top cover.

Temporary tack (from the center of the rail to the sides) to within 5cm/2in of the corners of the frame on the back, then the front and the side rails; tack off and fit the corners (p70). Trim the fabric to the tack line.

The outside back and arms should always be fitted last over a layer of batting and a lining of muslin or burlap. The lining is fitted to the frame in the same way as base burlap (p74).

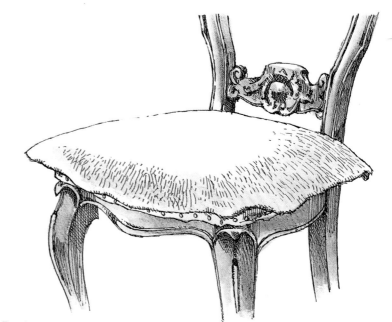

Batting

Back tacking strip can be used to fix outside panels to the frame, giving a neat finish and reinforcing the join (p157).

When stitching top cover use a small curved needle and thread to match the fabric. A good supply of upholsterer's pins or skewers is also useful. Use a small and neatly worked slipstitch (p69) to secure the fabric.

When working around curved shapes, snip the seam allowance to ease the fabric.

Slipstitching a seam

Fitting a pleat-tufted pad

Top cover is fitted to pleated tufting in a way similar to that for muslin (p100), but now the buttons are fixed in place.

I suggest that you have your buttons covered by a button-covering service. Alternatively, you could use a button press and follow the instructions.

Cut a 40cm/15in length of twine for each button tie. Cut a piece of polyester or cotton batting and place it on the pad; cut holes into it at the button points. Place the top cover on the pad. Thread a straight needle with twine, and, starting at the bottom row at a central button point, push the fabric into the dip and take the thread through the pad from the front. On the fabric side of the pad, thread a button onto the twine and then re-thread the needle on this side. Insert the needle into the pad again. At the back of the pad, make a slip knot and pull it tight around the rolls of muslin already tied to the previous button ties. Check that the button is nestling flat in the dip.

Work all the buttons, and then tighten the slip knots throughout and tie off with a double knot. Regulate the folds, tack off to all the rails, and trim the fabric.

Panels cannot be joined to pleat-tufted pads with straight seams, as

Tying-in a button to secure the top cover

this would show and the lines would interfere with the diagonal folds. Instead, the joining piece should be cut and folded to fit into the folds formed by the adjacent button(s) of the neighboring panel. The method is explained on p144. It is secured only at the button points; the join is not sewn.

Simple tufting

This method of finishing is a variant of the buttoning technique, but, unlike pleated tufting, it is done on the surface of the pad rather than cut into it.

Traditionally, tufts were made from short strands of silk, linen, or wool, but for general use today cotton embroidery thread is used. They are tied into little bundles like brush heads and then fixed to the pad with twines. (Tufts can also be used in the place of buttons on pleat-tufted pads; see p133).

The tufting technique can also be carried out with other materials: tiny ribbons, leather washers (such as those found on mattresses), decorative buttons, and upholstery domes. When domes are used in this way, the technique is known as float buttoning.

The instructions that follow are for tufts made with cotton embroidery threads on a simple stuffed pad with top cover fitted and tufting positions marked.

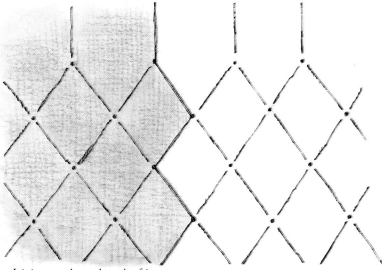

Joining panels on pleated tufting

1 Cut embroidery threads to a length of 4cm/1½in and arrange in bunches. Cut one piece of thread about 32cm/12½in long and loop it around the middle of one bunch, tying a slip knot tightly around it. Fasten with a double knot (a).

2 Fold the tuft over the center, holding it firmly between finger and thumb to splay it, and trim the edges neatly with sharp scissors. Cut the ties to the same length as the tuft (b).

3 Make all the tufts for the pad. Cut the required number of twine ties to fix the tufts in place. Thread a buttoning needle with one of the ties; insert it into the cover just slightly to one side of the tufting point and pull out at the back. Re-thread the needle on the top covered side, and take it back through the pad again, making a loop over the tuft (c).

4 Remove the needle and tie off with a slip knot, inserting a roll of muslin between the tie and the base burlap.

5 Insert the remaining tufts. When they are all in place, give them a final tightening and tie off with a double knot. They should be firmly anchored, but not so tightly that they strain the top cover.

6 Trim off any stray ends with sharp scissors and fluff out the tufts with a pin or skewer (d).

Attaching gimp

A gimp finish is used to conceal the tack line of the upholstery pad. It should be secured with a water-based glue and gimp pins that harmonize with the color of the trimming. If you cannot find the right color, you can paint the heads carefully with modeling enamel once they are in place.

1 Make sure you have a long enough length of gimp. Then start attaching it to the piece at a corner or near an upright rail. Turn under 1cm/½in and lightly glue the underside of the gimp. Secure in place with a gimp pin. As you work around the frame glue the gimp in place in 15cm/6in lengths and temporary tack with gimp pins (of any color). Make neat folds at any corners, if necessary, and follow any curves accurately.

2 Turn under 1cm/½in on the remaining end, and fix with a gimp pin. Press the gimp firmly in place all around. Finally, fix permanent gimp pins at corners or angles and joins, removing all the temporary gimp pins as you go.

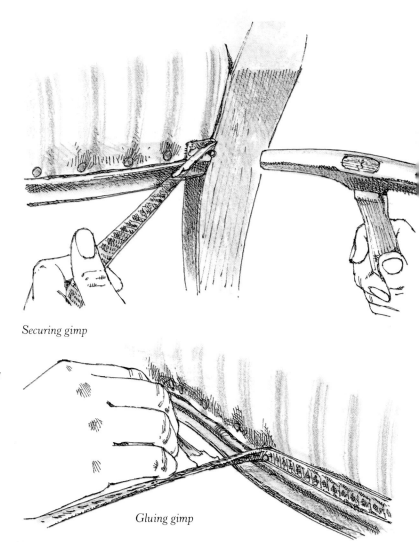

Securing gimp

Gluing gimp

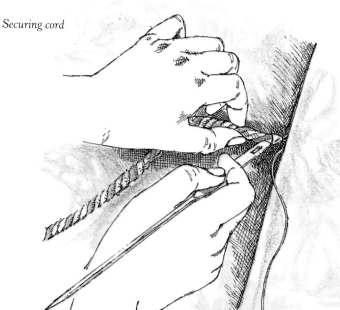

Securing cord

Sewing cord

Cord adds emphasis to the upholstery shape, along with a mood of opulence that cannot be achieved with the use of piping. Cords, braids, and fringes are all attached with slipstitches.

1 Seal the end of the cord with Scotch tape to prevent it from fraying. Thread a small curved needle with waxed thread in a harmonizing color; knot it to the end of the cord. If the end of the cord can be concealed between two pads, poke it well into the crevice and secure it with several knots. Or, if possible, tack off to a rail with a No. 10 tack.

2 Take 1cm/½in slipstitches (p69) along the cord to fasten securely in place.

About 5cm/2in from the end of the cord, seal it with tape and cut. Tuck into a crevice between the pads and secure with several knots if you cannot tack off to a rail.

Securing tassel cord and rosette

Slipstitching cord

Sewing tassels and rosettes

Tassels are sometimes sold attached to rosettes and can be secured to the chair or sofa by slipstitching around the rosette. If you have to stitch them separately, coil the tassel cord and stitch to the top cover before covering with a rosette and stitching in place.

Bottom lining

A bottom lining can be fitted to the base of seat frames to give a tidy finish and to collect any dust that may be shed by the upholstery materials. It is the final stage to be worked. Always used on sprung seats, it is optional on other pads.

Bottom lining is a black cotton fabric sold specifically for this use; it is usually cambric, but any other closely woven fabric that is darker than the top cover may be used.

Cut the fabric just a little larger than the frame and temporary tack all around, turning under the edge as you go, and cutting and fitting around the chair legs, so that the edge of the fabric is as near as possible to the inside of the rail. Tack off.

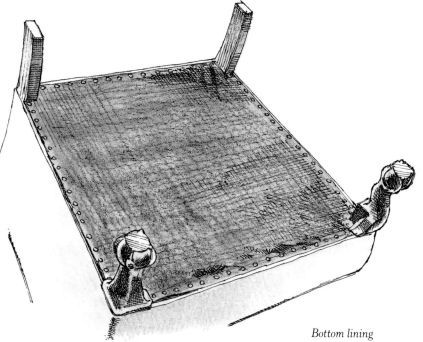

Bottom lining

THE
PROJECTS

Slip Seat

This is an excellent first project: a simple stuffed pad created on a seat frame which can be removed from the main frame.

I decided to cover the seat of this friendly 18th-century "country" chair in a strong fabric with a small oakleaf pattern. Woven horsehair, if available, would be a good choice if you wish to re-create the period style of this type of chair and is extremely hard-wearing. A subdued trellis pattern, a striped moiré, and a plain velvet were alternative fabric choices that I also considered.

The muslin covers of 18th-century seats were tacked off on the outside of the rail, as I do here, and in fact I always do this unless the fit into the main frame is too tight. On most modern slip seats the muslin is tacked off underneath the frame. If you wish to do this, follow the instructions for fitting the top cover (p121), but do not turn under the edges to finish them.

ORDER OF WORKING
Attach webbing
Attach base burlap
Insert bridle ties and stuffing
Attach muslin
Batting
Fit top cover

1 Attach the webbing (p72), using No. 10 tacks if the rail is strong enough (a). On a small frame use No. 8 tacks. Space the webs evenly, fanning them if necessary.

If you have difficulty holding the frame while straining the webbing, clamp it to your trestles with a C-clamp to stabilize it.

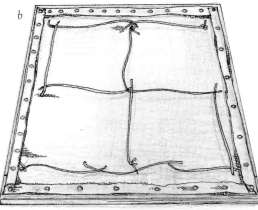

2 Attach the burlap (p74) using No. 8 tacks.

3 Insert bridle ties (p76) that allow for stuffing that compresses to about 3cm/1¼in (b).

4 Stuff into the bridle ties, molding a full firm center, thinning slightly to the edges (c). Press with your palms to gauge the density.

Remember that the edges will flatten when the muslin is pulled over them. They must not be sharp and bald along the top edge.

5 Cut a piece of muslin the size of
the area to be covered (from the
bottom of the outside rails) plus
8cm/3in on all sides. Fold in half to
find the center. Resting the frame
on the front rail, temporary tack the
muslin to the center of the outside of
the back rail (d).

Complete the temporary tacking
all along the back rail to within
5cm/2in of the corners.

6 Turn the frame so that the front
rail is to the top and the webbing
facing you. Tuck the frame under
your arm, and smooth the muslin up
and over, compressing it as you do
so with one hand while you pull the
muslin taut with the other hand.

Fix three temporary tacks to the
center of the outside front rail (e).

7 Turn the frame around and attach
the muslin in the same way to the
centers of the outsides of both side
rails. Check the tension of the
stuffing and muslin at this point (f).

8 Return to the center of the front rail and make sure that the edges are clean. Pull the muslin down over the rail, working it backward and forward with one hand as you ease the stuffing back to the top edge with the thumb of your other hand.

When the edges are smooth, temporary tack to within 5cm/2in of the corners. Temporary tack the two side rails in the same way (g).

Adjust any minor bumps with a small regulator or skewer.

Holes made in the muslin by the regulator can be smoothed over by stroking the warp and weft threads with the point of a skewer or pin.

g

9 When the edges are clean and you are happy with the shape, tack off throughout (h) before you work on the corners.

10 Pull the muslin down firmly over the corner, and adjust the stuffing if necessary to create a smooth line. You may have to remove a small amount of stuffing, as it will have been pushed along the sides (i).

Pull the muslin down firmly and tack along both edges to the corner (j). No corner fold should be necessary here.

h

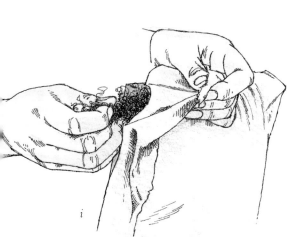

i

j

11 Cut away the excess muslin to the tack line (k).

Your pad is now ready for batting and top cover (l).

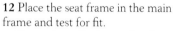

12 Place the seat frame in the main frame and test for fit.

Cut a piece of polyester batting to cover the top and just over the sides. If it is a tight fit, trim the batting back from the edge a little. Place the batting in position (m).

13 Measure for top cover at the widest and deepest point from the bottom of the outside rails, plus an additional 5cm/2in on all sides to allow for turning and tacking underneath the rails.

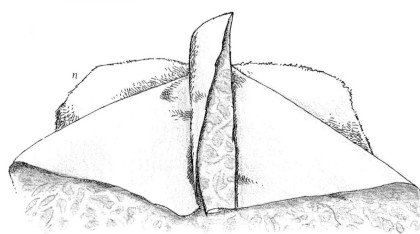

14 Cut out the fabric, fold it in half lengthwise, and pinch at the edges to mark the center front and back (n). (Fold in half widthwise and mark centers if necessary to help you to square the fabric.)

15 Measure and mark the center of all four rails on the sides with a pencil.

Place the top cover on the batting, matching the marked centers of fabric and rails.

16 Temporary tack on the underside of the back rail, about 1cm/½in from the outside edge, starting at the center and working to within 5cm/2in of the corners.

17 Pull the material over to the front, creating a firm but not overtight tension. Fix with three temporary tacks.
 Work the sides in the same way, making sure that the fabric is absolutely square (o).

18 Temporary tack along the side and front rails to within 5cm/2in of the corners.

19 Now finish the edges. Starting at the center of the back rail (p), turn under the material just below the temporary tacks, and tack off at the edge of the fold. Work along the rail, leaving the corners.
 Work the other three sides and remove the temporary tacks.

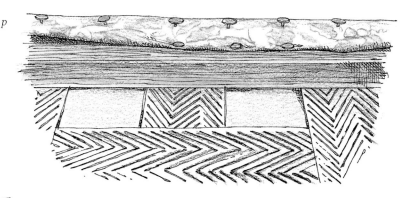

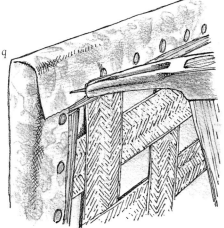

20 Fold and tack the corners (q and p70), with the opening of the fold on the side rails, tacking them underneath the rails (r).

21 The slip seat is now ready to be fitted into the main frame of the chair (s).

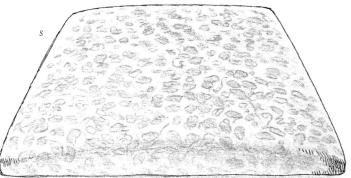

Drawing-room Chair

This pretty chair, in a style known as "rococo revival," has a double-stuffed stitched seat (p85). On this frame special care must be taken to follow the curved line, particularly with the edge stitching. Corners must be cut neatly to the upright rails for a smooth finish at all stages of working. The front corners of the chair have a double fold which creates a v shape complementing the cabriole legs.

The strong color of the show wood was taken into consideration when selecting a top cover. The fabric I chose has textural interest in its ridged grid-like pattern, which also helps with the fitting and alignment. An alternative classic choice for this type of chair would be a stylized floral damask pattern, with a large motif centered on the seat. I also considered two other fabrics with a ribbon motif which would be in keeping with the shape and the rather feminine mood of the chair.

ORDER OF WORKING

Attach webbing
Attach burlap
Insert bridle ties and stuffing
Tack scrim cover
Insert stuffing ties
Stitch edge walls
Tighten stuffing ties
Insert bridle ties into scrim pad
Second stuffing
Fit muslin
Batting
Fit top cover
Gimp finish

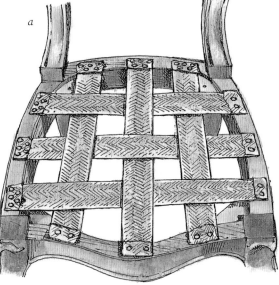

a

1 Fix the webs (a), fanning them out slightly on the front rail to cover the frame evenly. Use No. 10 tacks, and protect the show wood with padding when using the webbing stretcher.

2 Fix heavyweight burlap with No. 6 tacks. Insert the bridle ties about 8cm/3in from the rails, and stuff deeply.

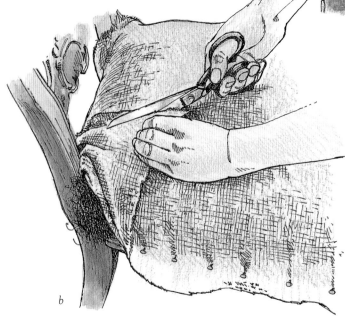

3 Cut the scrim. Tack it off on the back rail and temporary tack, using No. 4 tacks, to the front and side rails on the chamfered edges.

Cut and fit the corners at the back upright rails. Fold back the flap of scrim, and make a diagonal cut to within 1cm/½in of the inside corner of the rail (b).

b

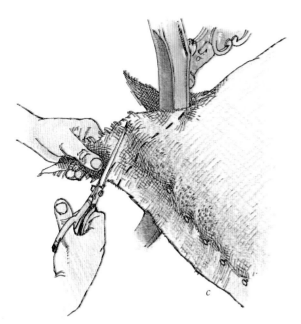

c

4 Test for fit by folding the scrim under to align with the front of the upright rail. If the scrim strains around the rails, clip a little closer to the rail. If you have cut too much and the stuffing bulges through, remove the scrim and reposition it about 2.5cm/1in back for a tighter fit at the corners.

When you are satisfied, crease the scrim down the fold line and cut off the excess fabric to within about 2.5cm/1in of the crease (c).

Fold the flap under itself so that the edge lies about 2mm/¹⁄₁₆in away from the show wood. Temporary tack in place (d).

5 Regulate the stuffing. Turn under the edges of the scrim on front and side rails and temporary tack. Fold and fit the front corners, then tack off all around.

Insert the stuffing ties. Regulate the stuffing at the edges of the pad.

6 Work the edge stitching with two rows of blind stitches and one row of top stitches on all the sides, paying careful attention to the front corners to ensure that they remain sharp and are not dragged around (e).

Tighten the stuffing ties (f).

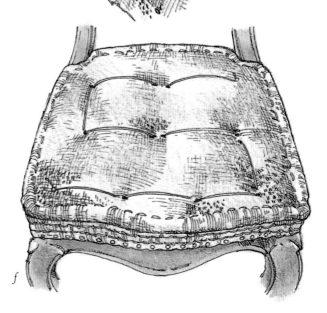

d

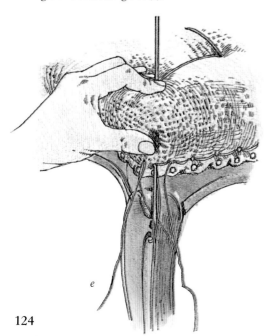

e

f

7 Insert bridle ties and make a shallow second stuffing of hair or fiber.

8 Cut the muslin, tack off, using No. 3 tacks, along the back rail, and temporary tack to the front and side rails.

Fit the corners at the upright rails, then fit the front corners.

Tack off the front and side rails and trim to the tack line all around.

9 Cut a piece of polyester batting, place on the seat and trim to 2.5cm/ 1in above the tack line.

Top cover and trimming

10 Measure the chair for top cover, and cut the fabric (p106).

Center the fabric on the chair and fix three temporary tacks (No. 3 or gimp pins) at the center of the back rail, turning under the edge 1cm/ ½in if the fabric is not too thick. Pull fabric to the front rail and fix with three temporary tacks, then work the side rails in the same way (g).

Trim the excess material to follow the shape of the rail.

Cut and fit the corners at the upright rails.

Continue temporary tacking the back, front, and then the side rails to within 5cm/2in of the corners, clipping where folds are created by the curves.

For the double-folded front corners, start by cutting away the excess batting (h). Pull the top cover down over the corner and tack (i). Cut away excess fabric on the lower edge. Draw the folds together to form a v shape and temporary tack in place. Do not turn under the edges to finish them, as this will create unevenness.

Tack off all the rails and trim to the tack line at the front corners (j).

Finish the chair by covering the tack line with gimp (p112).

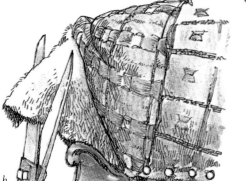

Leather-covered Chairs

These armchairs – known in England as carvers – are two of a set of dining chairs. When I came across them they were covered in a green woven fabric and I decided to restore their sagging upholstery and to give them a more stylistically appropriate hide cover.

A fabric with a strong stylized design (perhaps with a gothic or baronial feel to it) or a smaller pattern in a subtle, even somber mood, would enhance this type of chair, but avoid delicate fabric types and patterns, which would be not only inappropriate but also unsuitable for the wear that the chair will receive.

The upholstery is a simple pin-stuffed seat and back (p78) with a "wrap around" cover for the back. This is achieved by cutting both the muslin and the top cover in one piece, and by tacking off at start and finish underneath the bottom rail.

The seat has a "dished" shape, and I took care to preserve this by not over-stuffing the seat and by working the webbing and base burlap on the back and front rails first (although, of course, this is the usual order of working on most projects).

Leather is elastic and must be stretched tightly over the frame. It will show up any imperfection, so take great care at all stages of working, particularly in fitting the corners. Smoothly fitted, it will enhance chairs with clear straight lines. Brass nailing (below) is an effective and traditional finish to hide. Here, the heads of the nails are positioned so that they are just touching.

ORDER OF WORKING
Back
Attach webbing
Attach base burlap
Attach muslin and insert stuffing
Seat
Attach webbing
Attach base burlap
Insert stuffing and attach muslin
Top cover and trimming
Measure and cut hide
Fit the back
Fit the seat
Close nailing

Back

1 Using No. 6 tacks, attach a single vertical web to the center of the inside of the frame (a).

2 Attach burlap to the inside back, using No. 4 tacks and medium-weight burlap.

Turn the chair over and attach burlap to the outside back, with the edge folded to the inside for a smooth finish.

3 Felted cotton is used as stuffing here and is held in place with muslin, rather than bridle ties. Cut a piece of muslin long enough to wrap over the whole back with an additional 8cm/3in on all sides. Using No. 3 tacks, tack off onto the underside of the bottom rail. Turn the muslin back to allow for stuffing (b).

a

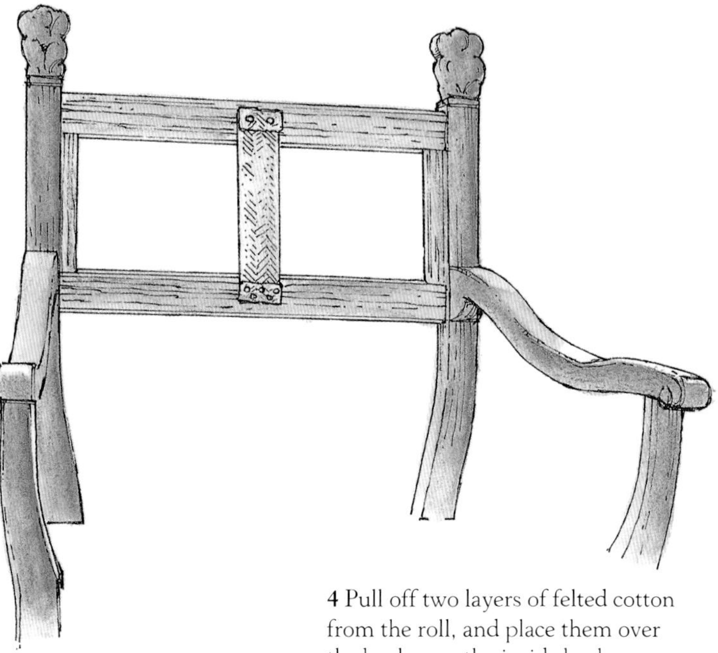

4 Pull off two layers of felted cotton from the roll, and place them over the burlap on the inside back. Handle the cotton with care to make sure that it remains smooth and intact – a jigsaw of pieces will give a lumpy surface.

5 Pull the muslin taut over the stuffing with one hand, smoothing firmly with the other. Temporary tack, using No. 3 tacks, to the top edge of the rail, leaving the remaining material to hang down the outside back.

Turn the sides under and temporary tack at the sides (c).

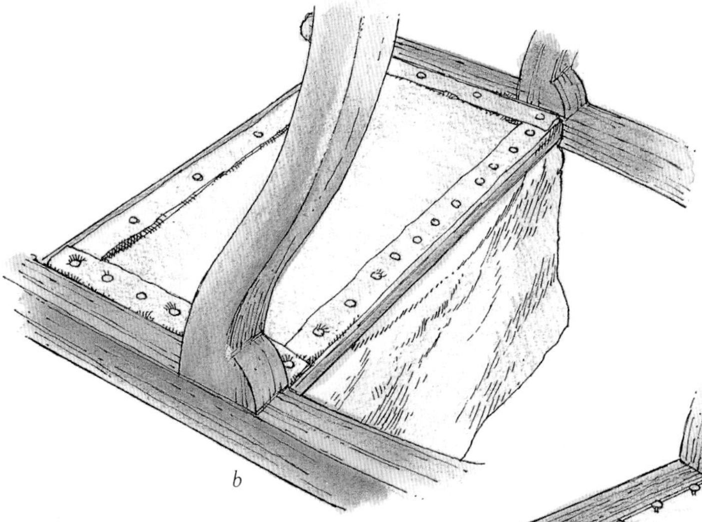

b

6 Turn the chair over and place one layer of felted cotton over the burlap on the outside back. Less padding is required here than on the inside back.

Pull the flap of muslin taut over the stuffing, and temporary tack to the bottom edge of the bottom rail and at the sides.

7 When satisfied with the finish, tack off all over, and cut off excess muslin.

c

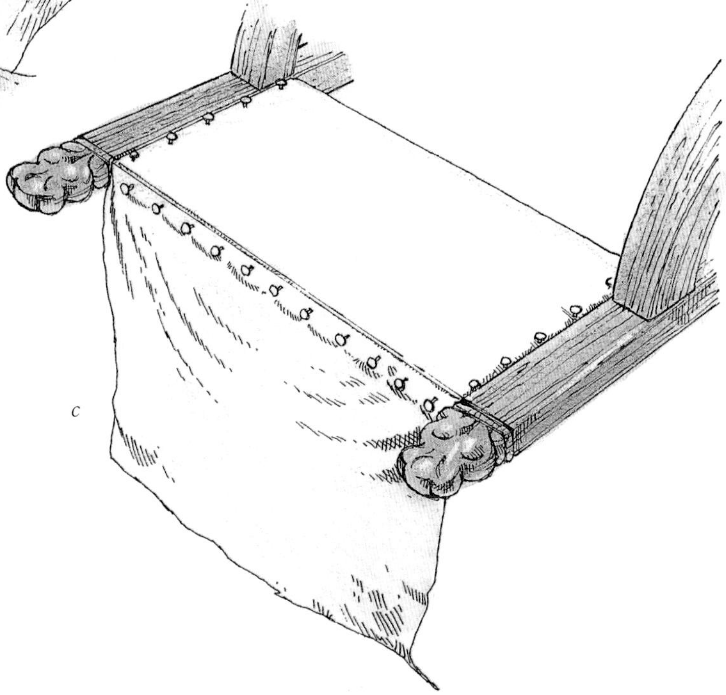

Seat

8 Web the seat, using No. 10 tacks and black and white webbing (d). When working on a dish-shaped seat such as this, fix the webs that run from the front to the back rails first. Do not distort the curve by tightening the interwoven lateral webs too much.

9 Using No. 8 tacks, attach heavyweight burlap, working from the back rail to the front to keep the shape.

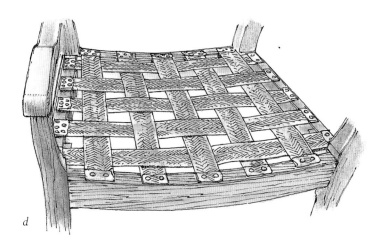

d

10 Put two or three layers of felted cotton on the seat, leaving a 10cm/ 4in gap around the edges. Feather the edges by pulling at them gently. Do not allow these layers of stuffing to create a domed look which would spoil the line (it is required to cope with the heavy-duty use the chair will receive).

Put two more layers of padding over the whole seat (e).

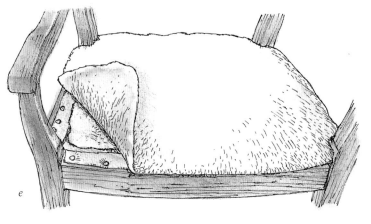

e

11 Cut a piece of muslin the size of the seat plus 8cm/3in on all sides. Using No. 4 tacks, tack the muslin to the outside of the back rail, about 2.5cm/1in down from the top edge, and work to within 5cm/2in of the corners. Pull the muslin over to the front rail, and temporary tack, making sure that the padding remains on the top of the seat, keeping a clean line at the rails. Temporary tack the side rails (f). Then work to within 5cm/2in of the corners on front and side rails.

12 Now cut and fit all four corners at the upright rails (p70).

Temporary tack close to the upright rails.

13 When you are satisfied with a firm, smooth finish, tack off and trim the muslin close to the tack line (g).

f

g

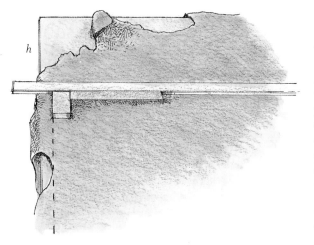

15 Top cover the back first. Tack the hide, using No. 3 tacks, to the underside of the bottom rail. Turn the chair and allow the hide to hang down while you fit the batting.

16 Cut one piece of polyester batting to fit over the front and back, leaving the sides clear, and hang it over the top rail.

Stretch the hide firmly up the outside back, over the top rail and down the inside back (i) and temporary tack to the underside of the bottom rail using harmonizing gimp pins over the previous row of tacks. Repeat, if necessary, until a very smooth fit is achieved.

17 Stretch the hide to the sides, and temporary tack with gimp pins (j). Remember that once punctured, the hole will remain and must either be trimmed away with a knife or hidden with close nailing.

Top cover and trimming

14 Measure for the top cover and add 8cm/3in to all measurements taken. Half a hide was required for a pair of these chairs.

Seat Measure at its maximum width and depth, from underneath the seat rails where it will be tacked off.

Back Measure from underneath the inside edge of the bottom rail, up the inside back, over the top rail, and down the outside back to the tack-off point underneath the bottom rail. Measure the width.

Check the polished surface of the hide for faults. Mark out the panels on the wrong side using a steel ruler or yardstick with a try square or right-angled triangle (h) and a pen or chalk. Cut the panels.

18 Trim away any excess hide underneath the bottom rail, leaving enough to turn under 5mm/¼in. Removing a few tacks at a time and working from the center, turn under and temporary tack. When you have achieved a neat straight line, tack off.

Tack off the sides and trim away any surplus hide with a sharp utility knife. The brass nails will cover the edge, so there is no need to turn under the edge.

19 Cut a piece of polyester batting to fit the seat, and place it on the muslin. Cut at the corners to allow for the upright rails.

Using No. 4 tacks, temporary tack the hide to the underside of the back rail, to within 5cm/2in of the corners. Strain the hide very firmly to the front, and temporary tack to the underside of the front rail (k). Temporary tack to the underside of the side rails.

20 Cut (l) and fit (m) the corners (p122-4) with care.

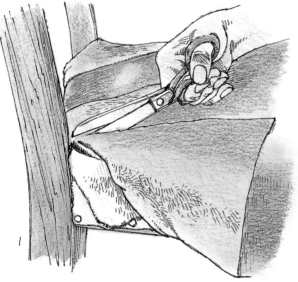

21 Tack off under all four rails (n). Trim away the excess hide.

22 Close brass nailing is the finishing touch. Hammer in the nails with the heads just touching, covering the gimp pins on the side rails of the inside and outside back of the chair.

Insert the brass nails at the corners of the seat (o).

Nails that are incorrectly positioned can be nudged into place from the side, or removed and repositioned.

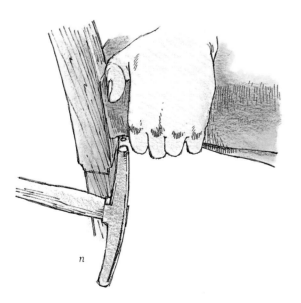

Late Victorian Armchair

The square back of this sturdy Victorian "Renaissance revival" armchair provides a suitable frame for a first project using pleated tufting (p98). A striped fabric may seem an ambitious choice because it could show up any errors, but in fact it helps with the alignment of the fabric on the pad. I decided to use tufts made from embroidery threads (p110) instead of buttons, for a softer effect and to finish off with banding and brass nailing to add an extra decorative touch to the serviceable mattress ticking.

The generous seat is sprung (p93) and then fitted with a firm double-stuffed stitched pad (p85). Great care is required at all stages when cutting around front arm support rails such as these.

The small armpads are also rather tricky to work, but patience will be repaid with good clean line and shape.

ORDER OF WORKING

Inside back
Attach webbing
Attach base burlap
Insert bridle ties and stuffing
Attach scrim
Stitch edges of pad
Mark buttoning patterns and cut
Layer felted cotton and polyester batting and cut
Fit muslin and button ties

Arms
Attach bridle ties and insert first stuffing
Attach scrim
Stitch edges of pad
Insert bridle ties and second stuffing
Attach muslin

Seat
Attach webbing
Plan, stitch, and lash springs
Attach base burlap
Stitch springs to burlap
Insert bridle ties and first stuffing
Attach scrim and insert stuffing ties
Stitch edge walls of pad
Insert bridle ties and second stuffing
Attach muslin

Top cover
Inside back: insert tufts
Seat
Arms
Outside back: fit lining and top cover
Bands and brass nailing

a

b

Inside back

1 Attach one jute web, centering it between the top and bottom rails, and another, also centered, from side to side; fix a medium-weight burlap using No. 6 tacks; insert the bridle ties (to allow for an edge height of 6cm/2½in).

2 Now work a pleat-tufted pad (p98) with a stitched edge to muslin.

For ease of working, tack off the scrim to the bottom rail before stuffing (a). Insert two rows of blind stitches and one row of top stitches, taking care to avoid scratching the show wood.

Mark the positions of the buttons leaving more space at the bottom than the top, so that once the seat pad has been worked the pattern is centered visually (b).

Arms

3 Tack hold (p69) two bridle ties to the arm rail (c) to allow for a 3cm/1¼in double-stuffed stitched pad (p85). Stuff very firmly. Fix the scrim to the inside arm rail with No. 4 tacks; pull over and fix to the outside rail. Tack off, and insert two rows of blind stitches and one small row of top stitches. Insert two bridle ties and stuff (d). Attach muslin (e).

Seat

4 Work a sprung base (p93) with a double-stuffed stitched pad (p85) to muslin stage. I used 20cm/8in, 10 gauge springs, arranged in three rows with three in the back row and four in the middle and front rows.

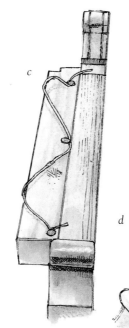

c

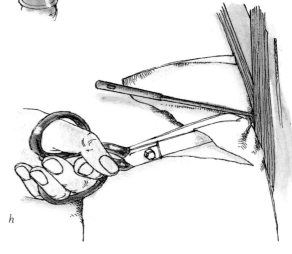

d

e

f

5 Insert three rows of blind stitches and one of top stitches, working the pad to an edge height of 8cm/3in.

The leg joint stands about 1cm/½in higher than the seat rail, so clip the scrim up to this point to fit and adjust the bottom row of stitching (f).

6 To fit the scrim and muslin around the front arm support rails, fold the fabric back when tacked to the front and back rails, and make diagonal cuts to form a v shape (g and h), using a regulator for accuracy. Tuck the flap under and tack the sides.

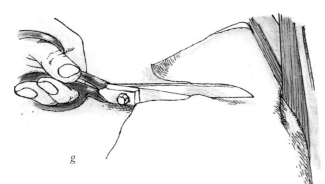

g

h

Top cover

7 Measure and cut out the top cover (p106). Make eight tufts (p110) and cut eight twine ties.

8 Work the inside back first. Cover with a piece of polyester batting, and cut the button holes through it.

Double check top cover measurements by centering the fabric on the pad and then pressing gently into the button positions along the length of the pad.

9 Now fit the top cover and tie in the tufts (i) in exactly the same way as muslin is fitted to a pleat-tufted pad, but threading the buttons (or tufts, in this case) onto the twine when making the ties (p110). Tie the twines over the existing twists of muslin on the back of the pad (j).

Start with one button point on the bottom row. Tie off the first tuft tightly, then follow a central thread in the fabric across to the next buttoning point to complete the row. Work the next row, encouraging the fabric to form diagonal folds into the buttoning points below, using a regulator if needed.

Outside back bottom rail

10 Complete all the rows, making sure that the top cover is taut and aligned.

Using gimp pins or No. 3 tacks, fold the pleats and tack off carefully at the sides.

11 At the bottom of the pad, push the fabric through the frame and pleat the excess fabric from the button points (k). Pull up and tack off to the bottom of the outside back, and trim.

12 Place one layer of polyester batting on the arms, and fit the top cover, making neat folds at the corners (l).

13 Cover the seat with polyester batting, trimmed to 2.5cm/1in above the seat rails, and cut around the upright rails.
   Attach the top cover, lining up the stripes with those at the center of the inside back (m).

14 The show wood at the bottom of the front upright arm rails had been damaged by tack holes from previous upholstery, so I had to cover them with a strip of material (n). Cut the fabric to fit around the front arm rail support. Tack all around and fit the corners (o).

Outside back

15 On the outside back, first attach a lining in the same way as for base burlap, using medium-weight burlap or muslin.

Cover with a layer of polyester batting.

Cut the top cover with an additional 2.5cm/1in on all sides. Center the fabric, turn under, and tack off (p).

Trimming

16 For the band finish, cut strips of fabric about 4cm/1½in wide on the bias and join as for piping (p169). Turn under the edges to form a band that is marginally wider than the head of the brass nails.

17 Turn under one end of the strip, and attach it to the corner of a rail with a brass nail.

Take the band around the rails, temporary tacking in place with gimp pins (q). Attach it with a brass nail at the corners and at the start and finish of rails.

Complete the nailing by inserting brass nails at 5cm/2in intervals. Where the rail will not divide exactly by 5cm/2in, make equal divisions along the rail.

18 Fold the band to follow the line of the show wood neatly at the corners (r).

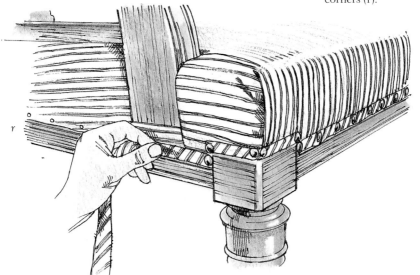

Iron-framed Armchair

This Victorian iron-framed nursing chair arrived in my workshop stripped bare, with all its original upholstery materials in two large bags. The evidence provided by the buttoned pad allowed me to follow the original buttoning pattern, and I was able to re-use some of the materials. The instructions that follow are for new upholstery throughout. For top covering, I chose a fabric with a delicate faded appearance which complements the mood of the chair.

The construction of iron-framed chairs gives them a long life, allows for the design of particularly beautiful shapes, and provides a certain amout of "give" in the back which adds comfort.

However, working the iron back is a lengthy business because all materials have to be pinned and sewn to the frame. This not only is more time-consuming than tacking but also makes the tension more difficult to control. Quite often, the iron work is rusty and needs to be wire brushed and treated with a preparatory rust-proofer to prevent it from eating through the base burlap. The rails should then be wrapped with strips of calico in order to prevent them from cutting through the materials.

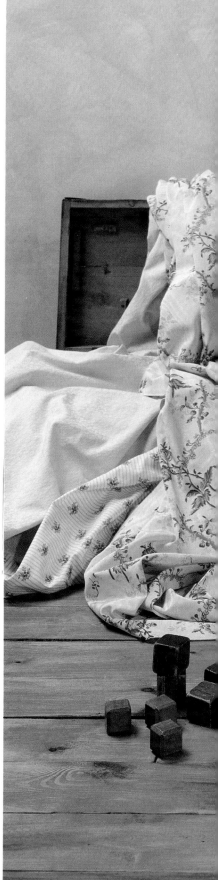

ORDER OF WORKING
Wrap metal frame with muslin
Inside back and arms
Fit base burlap
Stitch edge roll scrim and stuff
Work top stitches
Insert bridle ties and first stuffing
Fit scrim
Mark buttoning patterns and cut
Layer felted cotton and polyester
    batting and cut
Fit muslin with ties and stitch

Batting and top cover: inside
    back; inside arms
Seat
Fix webbing
Plan, stitch, and lash springs
Fix base burlap
Stitch springs to base burlap
Insert bridle ties and first stuffing
Fit scrim and insert stuffing ties
Stitch edge walls of pad
Insert bridle ties and second
    stuffing

Fit muslin
Batting and top cover
Outside back and arms
Fit lining
Fit top cover
Finishing
Attach gimp
Attach bottom lining

1 Wrap the rails of the metal frame.
Tear off long strips of muslin about
2.5cm/1in wide, and wind them
around all the rails, tucking in the
ends to secure them (a).

Inside back and arms
2 Cover the inside back and arms
with medium-weight burlap
(webbing is not required).
    Measure the width and add a
generous 37cm/15in on both sides
to allow for substantial shaping
darts. Measure the depth, adding
12cm/5in top and bottom.

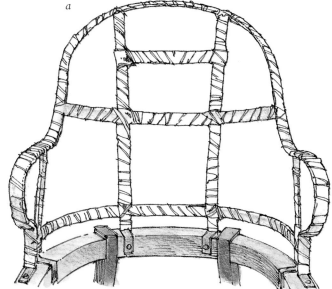

3 Cut and position the burlap,
anchoring it temporarily with
skewers at strategic points. Make
large cuts in the burlap where it
curves over the back and arms (b).
Begin shaping and fastening the
burlap to the frame by forming a
dart at each side of the base of the
inside back.

4 Now work methodically around the top of the frame, keeping the burlap taut and the weave straight all the time, snipping into the curves and pinning firmly all around the rails. Leave the arm fronts free at this stage (c).

5 Cut the burlap to fit it around the base of the vertical frame rails where they are bolted to the seat frame. To do this, insert the regulator, pulling the burlap taut at the rail point, and make a diagonal cut to each side of the rail, forming a v-shaped flap (d). Tuck the flap under and pull the burlap under the horizontal support.

6 With the burlap temporarily fastened to the frame, work around the outside back. Turn the edges under neatly, adjust the darts if necessary, and re-pin the burlap closely and firmly, ready for stitching.

7 To shape around the front arms, cut diagonally into the point where the base of the arm curve meets the upright support rail (e) and snip all around the curve, trimming away all excess material and pinning firmly at the back of the rails.

8 Thread a large curved needle with twine, and, working from the outside, backstitch the perimeter of the frame (f).

9 Now that the threads of the burlap running from top to bottom are fixed firmly by the pinning around the frame, the lateral threads can be tightened by securing the darts on each side of the frame with skewers. The inside arms and inside back should now be taut and run smoothly around the frame.

g

h

10 To pull the burlap into the shape of the back frame and to add strength, work a row of wide blanket stitches down the inside of both the vertical rails (g). (This will re-tighten the weft threads.) If there is not enough give in the burlap release the darts slightly. Then use small blanket stitches or backstitches to finish the darts.

11 Work a deep edge roll. Cut a piece of scrim about 1½ times the length of the top rail, measured from one front underarm point to the other (with a generous 12cm/5in allowance at both ends), and about 30cm/12in wide. Turn under about 4cm/1½in and pin in place on the inside back, about 8cm/3in from the top rail. (You may wish to draw a chalk guide line for this.) Making pleats to allow for the curve in the fabric, backstitch the scrim in place (h). Turn the scrim back to lie inside the frame, and stuff firmly to a depth of about 6cm/2½in. Turn the scrim over to the outside back of the chair and pin (i).

i

12 If the outside edge of the chair rolls out and over the rails as it does here, secure it with three rows of top stitches: one on the inner side of the rail, one almost above the rail, and a third just outside it.

Bridle tie the inside back and arms within the roll; stuff fully (j).

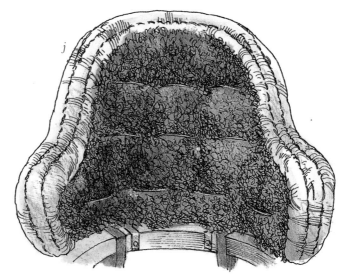

13 Measure for the scrim for the inside back (to be stitched at the top to the roll and at the bottom to the outside back rail). Make a generous allowance, as for the burlap (step 2). Cut to size.

14 Temporarily anchor the scrim in position with skewers, clipping around the bottom to release it and wrapping it around the rail (k). Fit and firmly pin it in place with skewers, clipping into it around the curve at the top and making darts as you did the burlap. Backstitch the scrim in place.

15 Work the pad to muslin stage (p 101-103), making sure that the rows of buttons follow through from the inside back to the arms (1).

The muslin is fitted in three pieces. Tie in the inside back first (m); then stitch the outside edges.

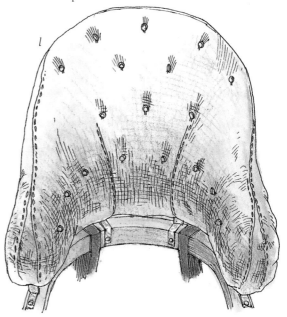

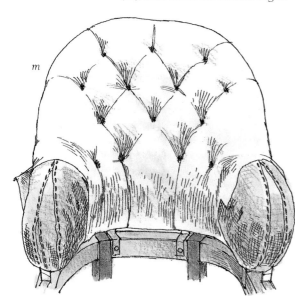

16 The arm muslin is joined to the back muslin by tying off at the button point on the bottom row as for top cover (step 18). Stitch the outside edges to the frame.

Top cover

17 Measure the inside back for batting and top cover. Measure the inside arms from the last button point on the inside back.

18 Fit the inside back top cover with buttons. (I decided to place a fruit motif within the dominant central diamond, and this determined my starting point.)

At the button point on the bottom row nearest the inside arm, tie the top cover into the hole without a button. Finally, complete the top row.

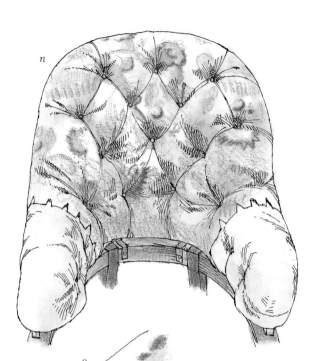

19 When all the buttons and button ties on the inside back are firmly tied off, pull the top cover over to the outside back and pin in place. Make tiny pleats on the outside back edge of the roll, fanning them neatly. Clip into the edges of the fabric at the inside arms to release the material to accommodate the curve (n).

20 Position the inside arm cover to overlap at the joining button on the inside back. You can insert this button first or, if you want to position the pattern of the fabric, tie off the two arm buttons first.

At the joining button, trim away any excess material, turn under about 1cm/½in, and button tie the folded edge into the hole (o).

21 Now pull the cover over to the outside arm. The edge of the inside arm cover will overlap that of the inside back. Clip into the material to allow for the curve (p). Fold under.

On the front curve of the arm, reduce the excess material by pleating on the outside, and pin (q).

22 Pull the bottom edge of the top
cover of inside back and arms
through to the outside and pin,
cutting around the upright rails,
smoothing the folds down from the
buttons. Backstitch top cover to
burlap all around the frame,
removing the pins as you go.

Seat

23 Work a double-stuffed stitched
pad (p85) with a sprung base (p93)
to muslin, building an 8cm/3in wall (r).

Fit the top cover. On rounded
corners, I would normally fit
double-fold corners (p131). Here,
to center the motif, I had to cut and
join fabric on one side and balance
it with a false seam. Where the
seams met the corners I
made a simple fold.

Outside back and arms

24 Fit the lining of burlap or muslin
in one piece, stitching to the frame
and tacking to the seat rail.

Measure and cut the top cover in
three pieces, allowing for a sloping
seam to suit the shape of the frame.

25 Layer with batting. Pin, then
stitch and tack the outside arm top
cover panels in place. Then pin and
tack the outside back, overlapping
with the edge of the arms. Turn
under and pin the seam (s). Stitch
and tack the panel in place and
slipstitch the seams (t).

Finishing

26 Fix gimp around the tack line of
the seat rail.

Fit bottom lining fabric.

Chaise Longue

This is a curvaceous sofa rather than a true *chaise longue*, but the upholstery is worked in the same way. Removal of a luminous pink nylon top cover, which was disguising the sofa's finer points, revealed an interesting conservation project. On all but the seat, the original pads, green damask cover, and cording details were intact so I decided to re-cover the smaller pads (below) over the top, in a complementary style. I replaced the seat with a double-stuffed stitched pad with a sprung base.

For the new top cover, I chose a traditional damask, rather gentler in color than the original green. I had planned to button before removing the cover but I discarded the idea because the leather washers I found along the top of the arm rail were not original to the frame, so I removed them and regulated the filling. Instead I added a little extravagance with a gathered border worked in a contrasting fabric. An unfaded strip on the edge of the old cover indicated that there had once been a border, and although I have no reason to think that it was either gathered or contrasting, this treatment is in keeping with the original style.

ORDER OF WORKING

Seat
Attach webbing
Plan, stitch, and lash springs
Attach base burlap
Stitch springs to burlap
Insert bridle ties and first stuffing
Attach scrim and insert stuffing ties
Stitch edge walls of pad
Attach muslin to back rail
Insert bridle ties and top stuffing
Attach muslin to front and side rails

Top cover
Cover all parts with batting
Inside arm
Top roll
Inside back
Arm rails
Seat
Gathered borders
Outside back and arm: lining and top cover
Attach cord, gimp, rosettes, and tassels
Attach bottom lining

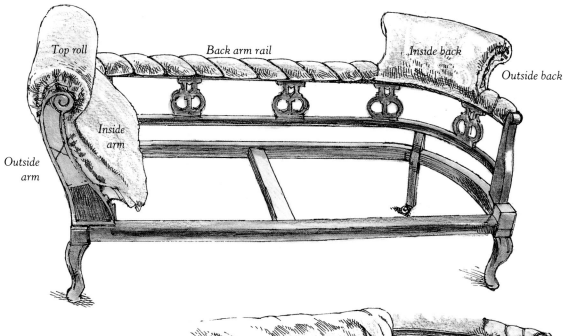

Top roll

Back arm rail

Inside back

Outside back

Inside arm

Outside arm

Seat

1 Work a sprung base (p93) with a double-stuffed stitched pad (p85).

Tack the muslin to the back rail (a) before inserting a light top stuffing to add comfort, but take care not to create a domed look, which would spoil the line.

Top cover

2 Measure for the top cover and draw up a cutting list (p106). Cut out and label the panels, remembering to center the pattern and follow it through on each piece. If the full width of the material is not wide enough for the seat panel, piece the cover at the open end and add a fly (p108) to the arm end. (Because a border will be added, the cover could be stitched to the pad at the top of the stitched edge to economize further if necessary.)

Measure and cut the borders, allowing 8cm/3in extra depth and about 2½ times the width, joining by machine as necessary.

3 Cover the inside arm with batting and trim to shape. Center the top cover. Using No. 3 tacks or gimp pins, tack it to the rail at the base of the top roll, using a regulator to hold the cover in place (b).

a

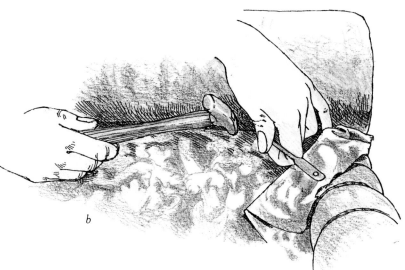

b

c

4 Pull the fabric down and temporary tack to the bottom rail. Temporary tack to the front of the inside arm rail, folding a neat corner at the bottom (c). Cut to the rail points at the back arm rail and temporary tack to the back of the inside arm rail (d). Tack off on all rails and trim to the tack line.

5 Cover the top roll with batting and trim to shape.

Center the top cover matching the pattern with the inside arm. Fold the right side of the top cover back over the inside arm; tack it to the inside rail at the base of the top roll, using back tacking strip.

d

e

f

6 Pull the top cover up over the roll and temporary tack to the outside rail at the base of the top roll. Temporary tack at both ends, folding the excess fabric into even pleats (e). Tack home and trim to the tack lines.

7 Cover the inside back with batting and trim to shape.

Center the cover, fold under at the bottom and temporary tack to the bottom rail. Pull over and tack to the outside of the top rail, then temporary tack at the sides, pleating smoothly around the curves (f). Tack off all over and trim to the tack lines.

8 Cover the long back arm rail with batting and trim to shape.

Center the top cover. Turn under and temporary tack to the front rail. Pull over, turn under, and temporary tack to the back rail, turning under neatly at each end. Tack off.

Work the short arm rail in the same way.

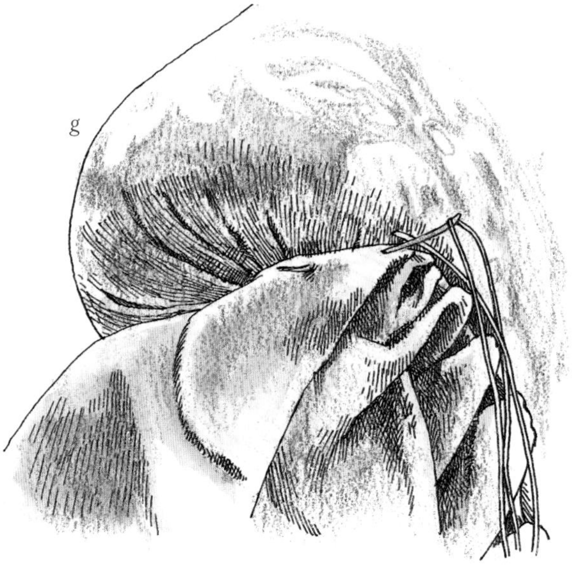

g

9 Cover the seat with batting. Center the top cover, temporary tack to the back rail, pull over, and temporary tack to the front and then at the side rails. Work a neat simple fold at the corner. Tack off and trim to the tack lines.

Gathered borders

10 Mark the stitching line for the borders with chalk. Thread a curved needle with waxed thread and knot the end.

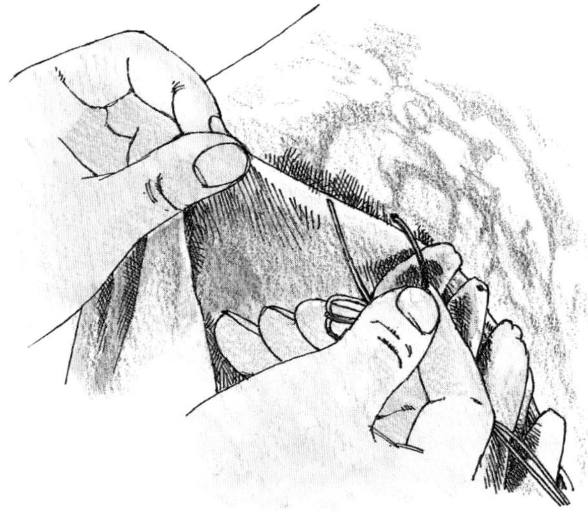

11 At the top corner of the border, fold under at the top and side. Insert the needle into the pad at the starting point and take a 1cm/½in stitch; pull the needle through, then insert it into the turned-under edge of the border and take a 2.5cm/1in stitch along the fold (g).

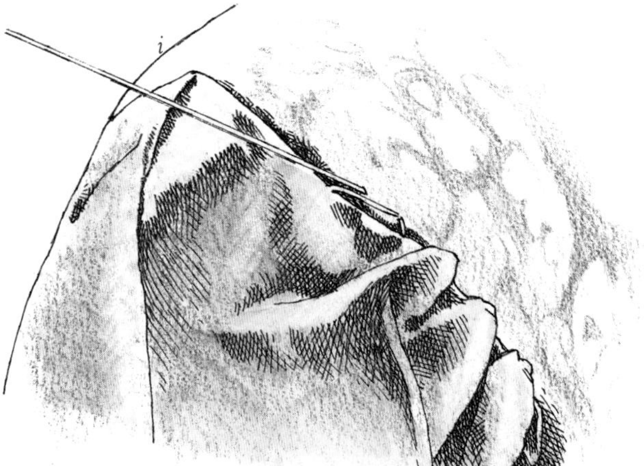

h

i

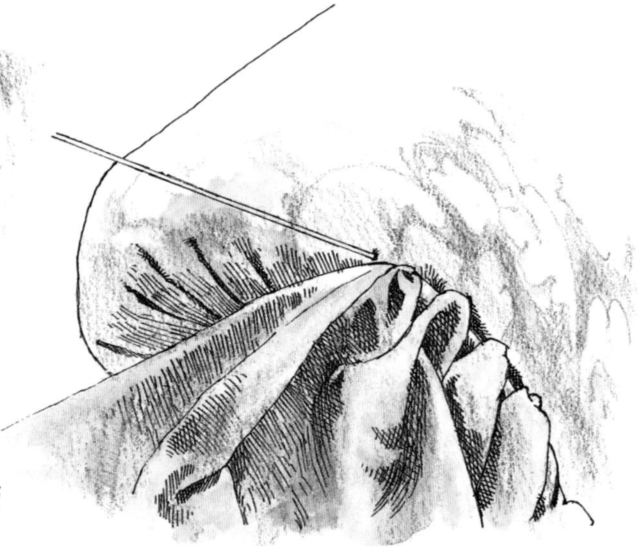

12 Return the needle through the pad next to the previous stitch (h) and take a 1cm/½in stitch along the border line, pulling through (i), drawing up and gathering the border onto the pad (j).

j

150

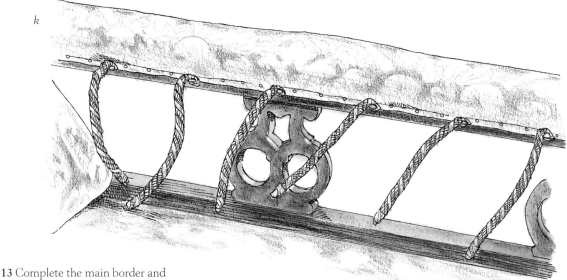

k

13 Complete the main border and the back borders in this manner, turning under at the end and fastening off with a double knot.

Pad the border with layers of polyester batting, using two on the back and arms and three on the seat. Pull the gathered border down and temporary tack to the rail, making sure that the folds have a random but neat appearance. The bulk of the fabric will preclude turning under at the show wood rail. Tack off and trim to tack lines.

l

14 Now fit lining and top cover on the outside arm and back.

Trimming
15 Stitch cord (p112) to all the relevant sections.

On the arm rails, apply the cord diagonally, following the indentations of the original cording pattern. Seal the end of the cord with clear tape and tack it firmly to the front rail. Pull over tightly and wrap tape around the tacking point at the back. Cut through at the center of the sealing tape. Repeat the process, tacking home all the cords at the front rail first (k). Then tack off all cords at the back rail (l).

m

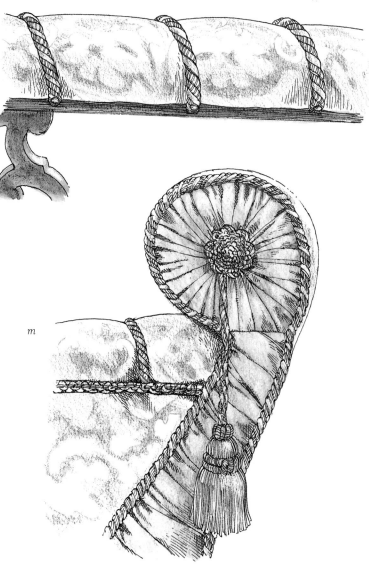

16 Attach gimp to all raw edges. For a luxurious touch, fix rosettes and tassels to both sides of the back and to the outside of the top rail (m).

Attach bottom lining (p113).

Edwardian Wing Chair

This Edwardian wing chair was the perfect vehicle for a richly faded, tapestry-effect fabric printed with peacocks which I was yearning to use, so I regarded it as a labor of love. Since the frame was very rocky, all the upholstery had to be removed and the joints strengthened before I could start re-upholstering.

If you have mastered the techniques of making a double-stuffed stitched seat with a sprung base, you will be proficient enough to cope with the complexities of working a wing chair. The project introduces working a deck of the type that is commonly used on sofas and easy chairs fitted with cushions. A row of springs along the front rail forms a sprung edge which gives additional comfort. (Note, however, that 18th-century chairs of this type did not have sprung seats and should not be treated in this way.) The project also involves making a gentle lumbar roll, which adds support to the base of the inside back of the chair.

By following the order of working that I used for this chair, and taking the seat to base burlap before working the back, wings, and arms from stuffing to top cover, you will provide a useful place to rest your tools as you work.

Inside back and wings

1 Attach webbing to the inside back; attach medium-weight burlap to the inside back and wings (a).

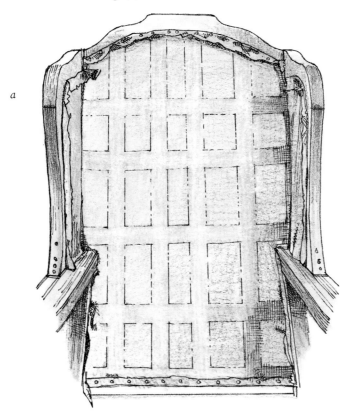

a

ORDER OF WORKING

Inside back, wings and arms
Attach webbing
Attach base burlap

Seat
Attach webbing, stitch and lash springs
Attach springs to front rail and lash to edge wire
Attach base burlap and stitch springs

Inside back
Fit lumbar roll scrim, insert bridle ties, stuff, and tack off
Insert bridle ties and stuffing on main area
Attach scrim all over, insert stuffing ties
Insert bridle ties and top stuffing
Fit muslin

Inside wings
Insert bridle ties and stuffing
Fit scrim and insert stuffing ties
Insert bridle ties and top stuffing
Fit muslin

Inside back and wings
Batting and top cover

Inside arms
Layer felted cotton and fit muslin
Batting and top cover

Arm tops
Layer batting and fit top cover

Seat
Insert bridle ties and stuffing
Fit scrim; insert edge and top stitches
Insert stuffing ties and stitch deck seamline
Insert bridle ties throughout and second stuffing into main body
Attach muslin to outside back rail
Stitch muslin to deck seamline and stuff deck
Complete muslin fitting
Batting, top cover and decking

Outside panels
Fit lining and top cover

Finishing and trimming
Make cushion and top cover
Attach cord and brass nails
Attach bottom lining

Inside arms

2 Tack webs to the rear and front of each arm. (The rear webs will support materials, since there are no back arm rails). Stitch base burlap to the rear webs (b); tack to the front rail (c).

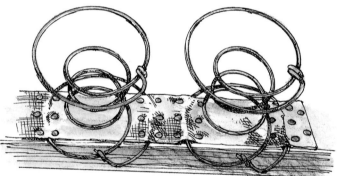

b

Seat

3 Attach the webbing and plan the springs (p93), allowing room for a row along the front rail to form the sprung edge. Stitch and lash the springs.

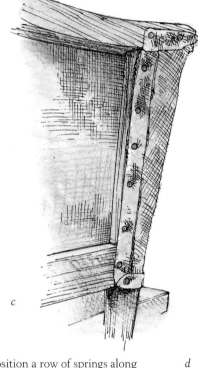

c

4 Position a row of springs along the front rail, fastening by means of a continuous strip of webbing tacked to the frame. Tack around the base coil of each spring to hold it firm (d).

d

e

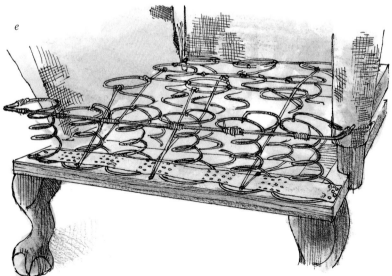

5 Cut a piece of edge wire to the length of the front edge, and bend it around the sides to follow the shape of the edge. Fasten, or "whip" (p97) the wire to the springs by winding twine along about 2.5cm/1in of the front of the top coil of each spring. Start with a slip knot, wind in the end, and finish with a triple knot. Whip the corner springs on both sides (e).

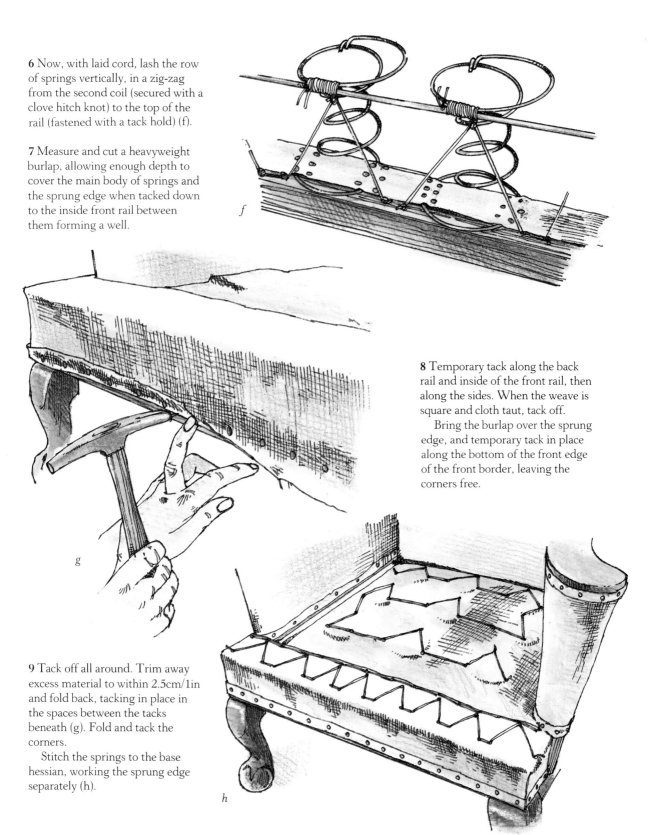

6 Now, with laid cord, lash the row of springs vertically, in a zig-zag from the second coil (secured with a clove hitch knot) to the top of the rail (fastened with a tack hold) (f).

7 Measure and cut a heavyweight burlap, allowing enough depth to cover the main body of springs and the sprung edge when tacked down to the inside front rail between them forming a well.

f

8 Temporary tack along the back rail and inside of the front rail, then along the sides. When the weave is square and cloth taut, tack off.

Bring the burlap over the sprung edge, and temporary tack in place along the bottom of the front edge of the front border, leaving the corners free.

g

9 Tack off all around. Trim away excess material to within 2.5cm/1in and fold back, tacking in place in the spaces between the tacks beneath (g). Fold and tack the corners.

Stitch the springs to the base hessian, working the sprung edge separately (h).

h

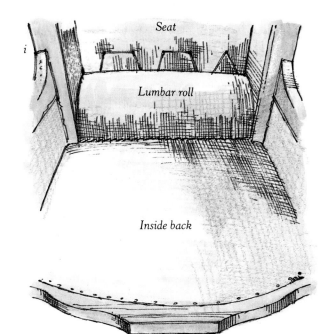

Inside back and wings

10 Work the lumbar roll. Measure from just below the top of the arms to the tack-off point on the inside bottom rail, for a pad 13-15cm/ 5-6in deep, allowing extra for turning under at the side and bottom rails. Cut the scrim, turn under, and stitch in place from side to side just below the top of the arms.

Fold the material back and insert bridle ties in the burlap lumbar roll area, then stuff fully. Pull the scrim tight, turn under, and tack to the bottom rail. Tack off at each side (i).

11 Bridle tie the main area of the inside back, and stuff to run evenly into the lumbar roll.

12 Cut a scrim to cover the main body of the inside back and stitch to the top of the lumbar roll, then tack it to the top and side rails. (Do not insert edge stitches – the stuffing should slope gently into the rail.) Insert stuffing ties (j). Insert bridle ties and top stuffing; fit muslin.

13 Insert one vertical row of bridle ties to each inside wing, tack hold to the top of the top rail. Work a double-stuffed pad to muslin (as for main body of inside back), but only temporary tack at the back rail.

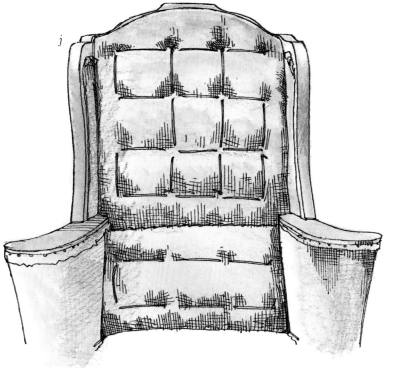

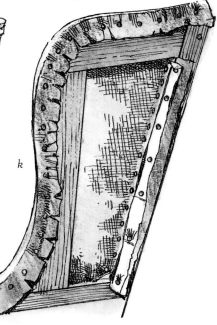

14 Now fit the top cover of the inside back and then the wings. The wing top covers will be tacked onto the outside of the arm rails. Use the regulator to find the cutting points where the wings meet the outside back, and snip to ease the cover around the curves (k). Tack off all the wing materials, finishing with the base burlap at the top.

Inside arms

15 Fill each arm with two layers of felted cotton, cover with muslin, and tack to the top of the arm rails (l). Layer with polyester batting, then fit the top cover, tacking again onto the top of the arms. At the join with the bottom of wing turn under and pin, then slipstitch.

Arm tops

16 Cut the top cover for one arm, making sure that the width allows for the curve. Position it, right side facing the inside arm, with the turning edge on top of the straight edge of the arm. Using back tacking strip aligned with the rail edge, tack to the frame (m).

l

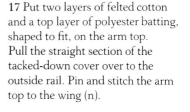

17 Put two layers of felted cotton and a top layer of polyester batting, shaped to fit, on the arm top. Pull the straight section of the tacked-down cover over to the outside rail. Pin and stitch the arm top to the wing (n).

18 To shape the arm front, trim the cover with about 2cm/¾in overlap, turn under and pin to the inside arm cover, ensuring a smooth line (o). Slipstitch all the seams in place. Repeat for the other arm.

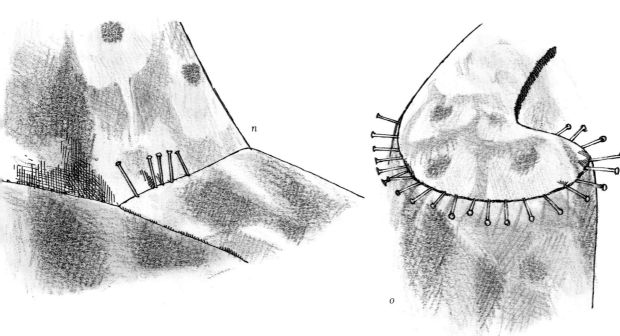

m

n

o

Seat

19 Bridle tie the burlap throughout (including the top of the sprung edge and the front border). Temporary tack the scrim to the back rail. Stuff the main body fairly lightly, but filling the well between the springs fully (p). Temporary tack the scrim to the side rails and pin to the top front edge of the front rail (q). When well fitted, tack off and, removing a few skewers at a time, turn under the edge of the scrim and re-pin it. Insert one row of locked blind edge stitches and one row of top stitches.

p

q

20 Insert stuffing ties in the main body of the seat and pull tight. Add the deck seam line of tightly pulled running stitches, about 18cm/7in back from the front, running from side to side along the well (r). Bridle tie throughout (including the front and side borders).

r

s

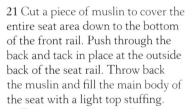

21 Cut a piece of muslin to cover the entire seat area down to the bottom of the front rail. Push through the back and tack in place at the outside back of the seat rail. Throw back the muslin and fill the main body of the seat with a light top stuffing.

Temporary tack the side rails, and pin the muslin along the deck seam line. When it is well fitted, tack off along the side rails and stitch the muslin to the deck seam line. Lightly stuff the deck and front border(s). Pull over the muslin and tack in place.

22 Cut the top cover, measuring from the deck seam line to the bottom of the front rail, allowing an additional 5cm/2in on all sides for tacking as usual and an extra 2.5cm/1in allowance at the seam line. Measure the body of the seat, adding the same allowance for turning under and tacking, and cut a panel of decking. Machine stitch the top cover to the front of the decking (t).

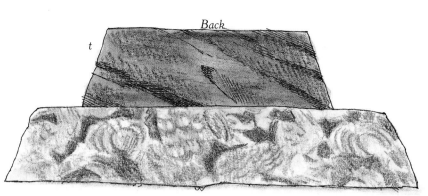

Back

23 Position the seam on the seat deck seam line and pin in place with the decking uppermost and forward. Fasten with running stitch. Cut and position a piece of polyester batting, and tack the decking in position at the back and side rails. Pad the front edge and tack the cover in place, making a simple fold at the corners.

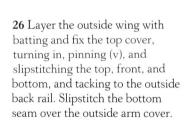

Outside panels
24 Fit a lining of burlap or muslin to all outside panels.

25 On the outside arm, tack the top cover along the straight section of the arm top using back tacking strip (u). Turn the cover back, apply a layer of batting and bring the cover down. Complete tacking along the top edge of the cover (at the bottom of the outside wing), turn under and pin at the front edge, tack at the outside back rail and the bottom rail. Slipstitch at the front.

26 Layer the outside wing with batting and fix the top cover, turning in, pinning (v), and slipstitching the top, front, and bottom, and tacking to the outside back rail. Slipstitch the bottom seam over the outside arm cover.

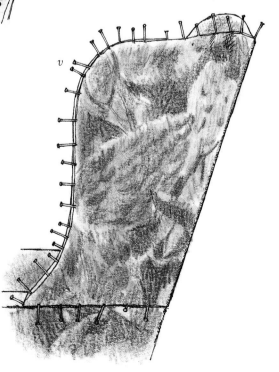

27 Pin the outside back in place, snipping to fit the curves of the frame top. Slipstitch in place and tack off at the bottom, under the seat rail.

Finishing and trimming
28 Make a boxed cushion (p102); fit with a piped top cover (p180).
  Stitch the cord (p112). Fix brass nails (p133) around the tops of the legs. Attach bottom lining (p113).

Chesterfield

This small chesterfield arrived in my workshop with sagging seat upholstery and, to my eye, a dull, restrained curve to the shape of the back and arms. I decided to re-upholster it on a grand scale, with huge sweeping curves, accentuated with cord and a fatly cushioned deck for comfort. The opulence of the colors and texture of the cover, as well as a tassel trim, further enhanced the grandeur of the finished effect.

I should give a warning here about upholstering chesterfields, for it is a major task – certainly something that a beginner should not undertake without the guidance of a teacher. The techniques that you will encounter are only slightly more complicated than those used for the wing chair project (p152). However, it requires patience, diligence, and sheer physical effort to deal with the size of the piece, and precision in planning and fixing the springs on the inside back and arms to create smooth lines. The deck is worked in a way similar to that of the wing chair, although there are differences in the way the front edge roll and border are stuffed to create a more robustly rounded effect.

ORDER OF WORKING

Inside back and arms
Attach webbing, stitch and lash springs
Attach base burlap and stitch springs

Seat
Attach webbing, stitch and lash springs
Attach springs to front rail and lash to edge wire
Attach base burlap and stitch springs

Inside back and arms
Insert bridle ties and stuffing
Attach scrim
Insert top stitches on outside edge
Insert stuffing ties
Stitch front arm roll
Tighten stuffing ties
Insert bridle ties and second stuffing
Fit muslin

Seat
Insert bridle ties and stuffing
Fit scrim; insert edge and top stitches
Insert stuffing ties and stitch deck seam line
Insert bridle ties throughout and second stuffing into main body
Attach muslin to outside back rail

Stitch muslin to deck seam line and stuff deck
Attach muslin to base of front edge roll
Attach muslin to front border and fill with felted cotton

Top cover and trimming
Inside back and arms: batting and top cover
Stitch cord to seams of inside arms and back
Seat: fit decking and top cover to base of front edge roll; fit top cover to front border
Outside back and arms: lining, batting, and top cover
Stitch cord to front seat edge
Arm fronts: felted cotton and top cover
Stitch cord to arm fronts
Sew on tassels and rosettes
Attach bottom lining
Make cushion and fit top cover

Inside back and arms

1 Attach the webbing, with a lateral web placed roughly equidistant between the top rail and the planned final height of the finished upholstered seat pad. Tack it to the outside of the rails, from one upright arm rail to the other. (Deeper frames require more than one lateral web.)

Attach the perpendicular webs about 18cm/7in apart (planning for the arrangement of the springs). Attach to the inside top rail, pass them behind the lateral web, and tack them to the outside of the bottom rail (a).

a

2 Stitch a first row of springs to the crossover points on the lateral web.

Then fix two rows to the top of the arm and back rails: one row on top, aligned with the first row; the other positioned in the spaces between the springs of the top row, leaning inward (achieved by bending the bottom coil over the inside edge of the rail) so that the springs slope with the curve of the arm. Secure both rows on the top of the rail with tacked webbing (p154). Secure the second row on the inside of the rail with hooped metal staples (b).

b

c

3 Lash the springs. Tack hold the laid cord at the inside edge of the top rail, knotting each top coil at opposite sides and securing with a tack at the outside edge of the rail. Next, lash the bottom rail perpendicularly to this top row. Then lash the sloping row from the top to the bottom rails. Lash all rows laterally from the front and back rails of the arms, and from side to side of the back (c).

4 Fix a heavyweight burlap to the inside back, folding in at the corners to make a pleat with the excess fabric. Fix burlaps to the inside arms at the top, bottom, and front rails (pleating to fit the curves on the front arm rails). Pin with skewers to inside back burlap. making a seam that follows the line of the upright back rail (d). Make sure that the burlap is taut, and join with a blanket stitch pulled tight to secure it. Stitch the top of the springs to the burlap.

d

Seat

5 Work a sprung seat to spring-tied base burlap (e) as for the wing chair, p154, steps 3-9.

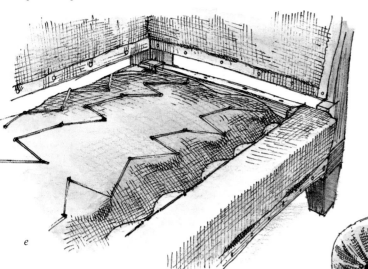

e

Inside back and arms

6 Insert large-looped bridle ties, including two rows along the outside edge of the arms and inside back. One row of bridle ties will be enough for a slimmer shape.

Stuff very fully and firmly into the bridle ties (f).

Attach the inside back scrim to top and bottom rails. Fix the arm scrims to the bottom, top, and front rails (g); pin them tautly to the back scrim as for the base burlap. Then blanket stitch in place.

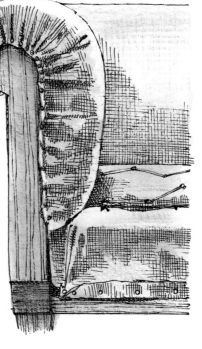

f

g

7 Insert one row of top stitches on the outside edge of the arms and back, to shape a large, fat edge roll on the outer curve (h).

Insert stuffing ties into the inside back and arms.

8 Now build up the front arm edge with stitches to create a roll standing proud of the front scroll. Work three rows of blind stitches and one of top stitches, tapering them into one row at both the start and the finish (i).

9 Tighten the stuffing ties, insert bridle ties and the second stuffing, then fit the muslin, in the same way as the burlap and scrim but joining the seam with slipstitch.

h

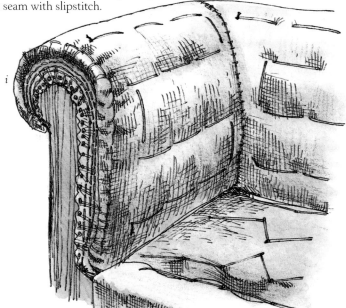

i

Seat

10 Work the seat until the deck seam line is stitched to the pad at muslin stage as for the wing chair (p158, steps 19-21), but work the front differently, as follows.

Do not insert bridle ties into the base burlap on the front border. Stuff firmly into the deck muslin to create a generous shape, and backstitch the muslin below the edge roll to secure it.

The fullness in the lower part of the front border is created by filling with four layers of felted cotton, encased by a separate piece of muslin which is stitched below the edge roll and tacked off underneath the front rail and at the sides on the arm fronts (j).

j

Top cover

11 Measure for the top cover and draw up a cutting list (p106), noting method in step 13 for working a separate front panel.

12 Cover the inside back and arms with batting and trim to size.

Fit the top cover in the same way as the muslin, snipping the curve as necessary. Secure the pleats around the front curves of the arm and the curve of the back with skewers before stitching in place (k). Trim off the excess fabric.

Stitch the cord to the seams of the inside arms and back (p112) and fasten with a tack hold at each end of the cord.

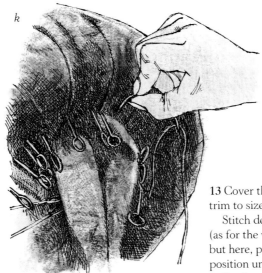

13 Cover the seat with batting and trim to size.

Stitch decking to the top cover (as for the wing chair, steps *22-23*) but here, pin (l) and then stitch in position under the front edge roll, as for the muslin (step 10). Backstitch the top edge of the front border under the front edge roll. Layer batting, pull down the top cover, and tack under the bottom seat rail, then tack to the front of the arm upright rails.

14 Fix lining (of medium-weight burlap or muslin) to the outside arms and back. Cover with batting and cut to size.

15 Fit the top cover to the outside arms, using back tacking strip at the top rails (p159) and tacking off under the bottom rails. Tack off on the outside edges of the front and back arm rails.

16 Fit the top cover of the outside back in the same way, but slipstitch to the arm panels at the back rail edges, covering the tacks.

17 Before working the arm fronts, first slipstitch the cord along the front seat edge, tacking off each end with a No. 10 tack on the front upright arm rails.

18 Position three layers of felted cotton on the arm front and trim to shape. Turn under 1-2.5cm/½-1in all around the top cover, snip to ease around the scroll curves, and pin. Slipstitch in place.

Stitch cord around the front panels (m). Sew the tassels and rosettes in place.

19 Fit the bottom lining.

20 Make a cushion (p102) and fit a piped top cover (p181).

Slipcovers

The techniques involved in making slipcovers are very different from those for fitting top covers to fixed upholstery. The removable covers are carefully fitted and sewn, so basic dressmaking skills are needed. A sewing machine is an essential piece of equipment.

The pieces are fitted on the chair right side out (with wrong sides pinned together), so that patterns, if any, can be matched. When joining seams, professionals simply pin and stitch, as shown here. However, if you are learning the craft, you should baste the pieces together just before stitching (*not* during the fitting) to ensure that all layers remain positioned correctly. Finish seams as you go, using an overlocking or zigzag stitch, or trimming with pinking shears. Try to avoid joining pieces at the front, not only for the sake of appearance, but also to avoid wear. Always take great care to ease piping for a good fit.

The first project demonstrates how slipcovers can give new life to very ordinary chair frames, while the second explains the more traditional treatment used for cushioned chairs and sofas.

MATERIALS & EQUIPMENT
Chairs and sofa
Fabric
Narrow pre-shrunk filler cord
Fastenings: Velcro (2.5cm/1in wide), nylon zipper, snaps, or hooks and eyes
Strong sewing thread
Tape measure, ruler, and right-angled triangle
Tailor's chalk or dressmaker's pencil
Steel pins
Scissors
Sewing machine
Sofa only
Brown paper for cushion template
Lining fabric

Breakfast-room Chairs

This project is a simple introduction to the basic techniques for making slipcovers. The chair has no awkward angles and no arms or cushions to be covered, and the skirt is simply gathered. Instructions for a skirt with inverted pleats are also given.

ORDER OF WORKING
Take measurements
Cut out pieces
Fit inside back
Fit seat
Fit seat border
Fit outside back
Make piping
Join and pipe seams
Make and attach skirt
Attach Velcro fastening

Chair with gathered skirt
1 Take the measurements shown on the diagram and add an extra 5cm/2in throughout, unless otherwise stated (to allow for tuck-ins, etc.)
Inside back (A) plus 7.5cm/3in; (B).
Seat (C) plus 7.5cm/3in; (D).
Outside back (E) from top edge of back to lower edge of seat rail where skirt seam will join; (B) plus 10cm/4in to include center opening.
Border (F) also measure length all around the seat.
Skirt (G) from lower edge of seat rail plus 7cm/2¾in. Width depends on the desired amount of fullness and varies from one-and-a-half to two times the finished width; heavier fabric requires less fullness.
Piping Measure distance around seams to be piped. Add 1cm/⅜in per join and about 25cm/10in to the total.

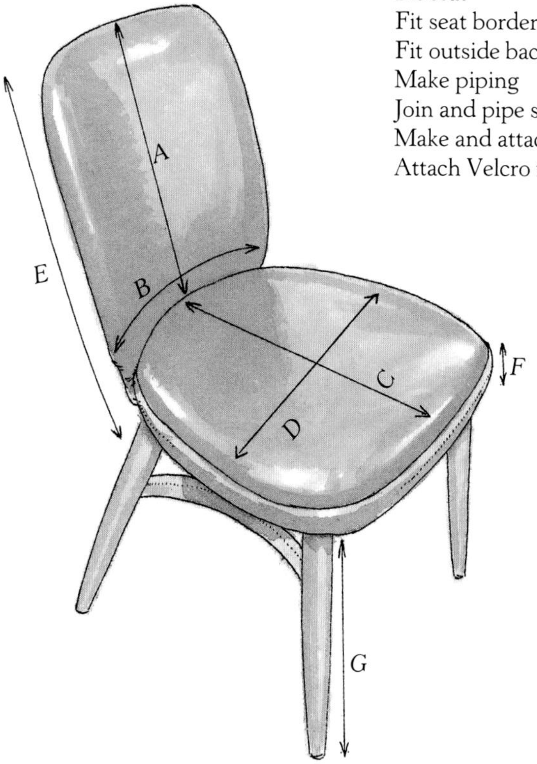

2 Draw up a cutting list (p106) based on the above dimensions. Draw a small scale plan of the pieces, fitting them into the represented width of fabric and remembering to position the lengthwise dimensions along the length of the fabric. The skirt needs to be divided into two or more pieces. Indicate the strips for the piping, which should be cut at a 45° angle to the grain. For economy, these need to be pieced – but joins should be at least 40cm/16in apart, and, allowing for the diagonal cutting, this would require an additional 30cm/12in of fabric. However, strips can often be fitted into spaces left around other pieces. You may also need to buy extra if matching patterns; ask the salesperson to advise on quantities.

3 Mark the pieces on the fabric with chalk or dressmaker's pencil, using a ruler and triangle. Cut them out; do *not* tear along the grain, which could distort the edges. If the fabric has a pronounced pattern, remember to position motifs as you wish them to appear in the finished cover. Patterns may also need to be matched at the seams.

4 Cut the strips for the piping; the width should be the circumference of the cord plus 4cm/1½in for seam allowance.

a

b

c

Seat

Border

5 Fit the inside back to the chair, with the fabric right side out. If the chair is upholstered, pin into the seams; here fine pins are inserted into the plastic. Smooth the fabric to fit the shape; avoid pulling it straight across. At least 2.5cm/1in should extend at top and sides. Do not trim. Using the ruler, poke the tuck-in allowance into the crease (a).

Fit the seat to the chair in the same way.

6 Fit the border under the seat piece, matching the fabric pattern, if any, all around. Pin the seat piece and border together, wrong sides facing, following the line of the chair (b).

Trim the fabric edges to 2cm/¾in all around. Cut wide notches at intervals for matching later (c).

7 Pin the outside back to the chair, leaving 2.5cm/1in at the sides and top; there will be excess fabric in the center for the opening. Fit and pin the inside and outside backs together as in step 6. Fit the end of the border to the outside back.

8 At center back, pin the edges of the fold together, following the shape of the chair. Cut down the center of the fold, then trim the edges to 2.5cm/1in; notch. Trim the curved edges of the back to 2cm/¾in and notch (d).

9 Mark the depth of the skirt seam line on the border all around using pencil or chalk. Trim the edge to 2cm/¾in outside this line.

10 Pull out the tuck-ins of the inside back and seat, and pin them together, taking 2cm/¾in seam allowance. Notch at the center.

11 Unpin the center back opening, and ease the cover off the chair. Leave the cover pinned together. When joining sections (steps 14-20), turn them with right sides facing, remembering to match notches.

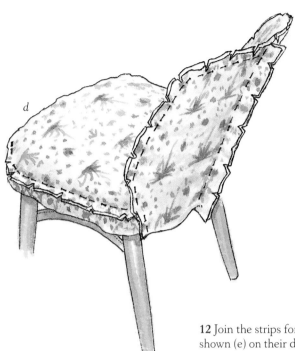

d

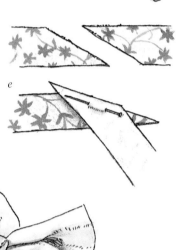

e

12 Join the strips for the piping as shown (e) on their diagonal edges (straight grain), taking 1cm/⅜in seams. Press the seams open and trim the protruding corners. Cut the whole piece into the lengths required for piping each seam.

13 Wrap the fabric strip around the cord, right side outside, and stitch close to the cord, using the zipper foot and a medium-long stitch.

14 Pin, baste, and stitch the tuck-in seam, with right sides facing and notches matching. Press the seam flat, *not* open.

15 Pin and baste piping to the lower edge of the border, first cutting back the cord by 2.5cm/1in to reduce bulk at the side seam (f). Cut the cord at the opposite end in the same way.

16 Pin and baste piping to edge of seat, with raw edges matching. Cut back cord as before, and ease the piping around the curves.

17 Pin (g), baste, and stitch the border to the seat edge, enclosing the piping and matching notches. Stitch through all thicknesses, close to the cord. Trim excess piping fabric at side seams. Press seam toward seat.

f

Seat

Border

g

Top edge

18 Join the top of the center seam of the outside back for 5cm/2in. Press the seam toward the right-hand side.

19 Attach piping to lower edges of outside back pieces as in step 16. Pin and baste piping to long outside back edge, easing it around curves.

20 Join the inside back and outside back sections, as in step 14. Press the seam toward the back. All the seams have now been piped and joined (h) and are ready for the skirt to be attached.

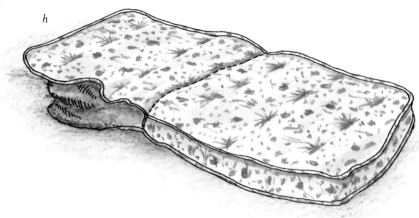

h

21 Now make up the skirt. If two fabric widths are being used cut one in half lengthwise and stitch these pieces to each side of the other piece so that a seam will not fall at the center. Press the seams open. Turn up and machine stitch a double 2.5cm/1in hem along the bottom edge.

22 Divide the lower edge of the seat cover into four equal sections. Pin the skirt to this edge, with right sides facing, and gather each section to fit. Adjust the gathers evenly. Pin at short intervals, baste, and stitch, using the zipper foot and working on the gathered side close to the piping. Smooth out the gathers with a small skewer as you work. Press the seam upward.

23 Pin the hooked side of the Velcro to the left-hand edge of the opening, placing the left edge of the Velcro 2.5cm/1in from the edge, and turning under 1.5cm/½in at the upper and lower ends. Stitch in place along both long edges. Trim away the seam allowance close to the stitching.

24 Pin and stitch the furry side of the Velcro to the right-hand seam allowance along its right-hand edge (placed 2.5cm/1in from the fabric edge). Trim the seam allowance close to the stitching to reduce bulk. Where the two pieces of Velcro meet at the upper end, overcast them together (i).

25 The cover is now complete. Press it carefully. Slip the cover over the seat and press the two pieces of Velcro together (j) to fasten.

Tuck the fabric down into the back of the seat to ensure a smooth finish.

For a final decorative touch, you may like to tie some bows of ribbon or fabric, and stitch them to the corners of the seat.

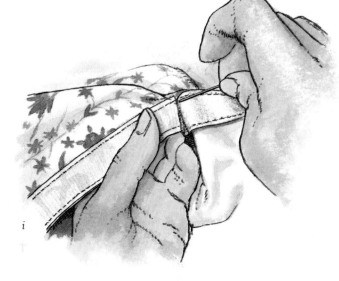

i

j

Cover with pleated skirt

The back and seat of this cover are made in the same way as the one with the gathered skirt, following steps 1-20. The cutting out of the skirt requires more planning. Ideally, it should be made first in cheap fabric, and then taken apart and used as a pattern. Alternatively, the positioning of the pleats and seams can be calculated by attaching a length of woven tape to the center front of the frame and marking these points on the tape.

It is important to place seams inside the pleats, preferably at the center of the pleat, right at the chair leg. It is important also to match any pattern as closely as possible; this is relatively easy at the front, but can be tricky at the sides, after the pleats are formed. It is best to cut the pieces generously to allow for this.

1 Measure and cut the front section of the skirt, two side sections and two back sections, adding 2.5cm/1in to each edge for seam allowance and 5cm/4in (or desired amount) for the pleat. Omit pleat allowance at center back. Pin, baste, and stitch seams, and press them open. Make a double 2.5cm/1in hem on the lower edge as for the gathered skirt, step 21.

k

l

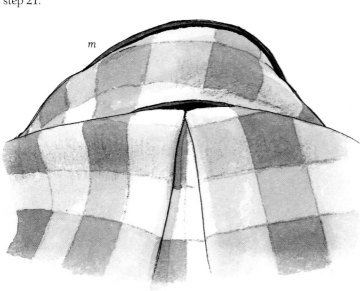

m

2 Mark the positions of the chair legs on the piped border. Pin the skirt to the border, starting at the center front, and work toward one leg. At the corner mark, fold the fabric back 5cm/2in (or the depth of the pleat) and pin it in place, then fold it forward (k). Make another fold the same size, bringing the inner fold close to the opposite one (l) to ensure that they meet exactly (m). Pin the pleat firmly in place. Continue around to the center back, then pleat the other side in the same way.

3 At the center back, trim away any excess fabric to align with the outside back edge of the cover.

4 Baste and stitch the skirt close to the piping. Complete the cover as in steps *23-25* of the gathered skirt version.

Three-seater Sofa

Making slipcovers for a large sofa is a major undertaking and requires a good command of sewing skills. If you wish to start on a smaller scale, the method for planning and fitting the covers can be adapted for armchairs and wing chairs (in which case, it is unlikely that you will need to join the fabric on the seat and back as was necessary here).

In spite of the ragged appearance of this sofa when I found it, the upholstery was sound. Nonetheless I decided to give it a new jacket of muslin over the old materials and to make new feather-filled cushions (p102).

A bright floral fabric is ideal for a summery effect. Another set of covers could be made in a more subdued pattern and color for the winter; being removable – for variety and for drycleaning – is the main advantage of slipcovers.

Estimating the fabric and planning the fall of a patterned fabric is the same as for top covering fixed upholstery. Having made your cutting plan, add a generous overall allowance (particularly at the tuck-in points) before buying the fabric. In general, slipcovers should fit snugly; however, at certain stress points, notably the front of the arms, a little ease is required. In fitting, therefore, a extra wide seam allowance may be taken, but when seaming, the normal allowance (here 2cm/¾in, except where otherwise specified) applies.

The method of covering cushions, described on pp180-1, is exactly the same for both slipcovers and fixed covers. The seams of the borders are piped, or corded, and there is a zipper at the back.

You can cut all the pieces from your cutting plan before you start fitting the covers, or cut as you work on the piece, as described below.

ORDER OF WORKING
Fit seat
Fit inside back
Fit inside arms
Fit outside arms
Fit outside back
Fit scroll arms
Make skirt and piping
Join and pipe seams
Fit skirt
Join and line skirt
Attach Velcro fastening
Cover cushions

a

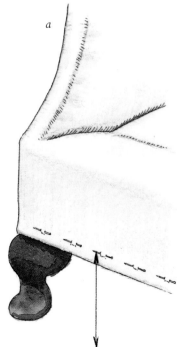

1 Measure the depth of the skirt from the floor up to 2.5cm/1in above the bottom rail, and mark this position with pins all around the frame (a).

Seat

2 Trim the edge of fabric to ensure that it is straight. Place the roll on the sofa, centered, adjusting it if necessary so that the pattern is positioned as desired (b). Measure the depth of the seat to the pin line and add tuck-in and front seam allowances. Cut two pieces to this measurement, matching the pattern, if necessary. Stitch them right sides together down both sides along the selvages, forming a giant ring. Cut vertically through the center of one piece and open out.

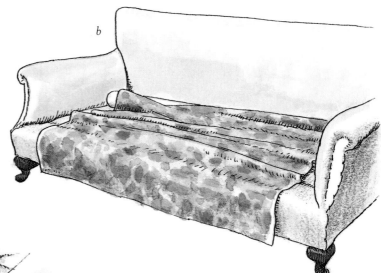

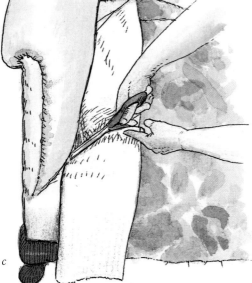

3 Measure the width of the seat, and mark the center with a pin near the front edge. Find the center of the seat fabric, and align this with the pin. Smooth the fabric over the seat, anchoring it with pins, and tuck it under the left arm as far as possible. Fold the fabric back, and measure the distance from the fold to the outside edge of the sofa. Add this measurement, plus seam allowance, to the folded-back edge, then cut straight back to the top edge of the fabric. Trim the excess fabric at the top corner in a curve to reduce bulk. Repeat step 3 at the other side of the sofa.

4 Find the point at the front of the arm where the tuck-in disappears, and mark the fabric at this point. Cut diagonally, almost to the mark (c). Tuck the fabric in all around the seat back and sides (d); the fitting at the corners will be done later.

Inside back

5 Measure the inside back depth from the seat up to the seam at the top, and add seam and tuck-in allowances. Cut two pieces of fabric to this measurement, and join them as described for the seat (step 2).

6 Center the inside back piece over the sofa, and fold the fabric back along the right-hand seam. Measure from the side edge to the stitching (e) and add outer seam allowance. Cut the side panel straight along this measurement to the bottom. Trim corner in a curve, as before. Repeat step 6 at the other side of the sofa.

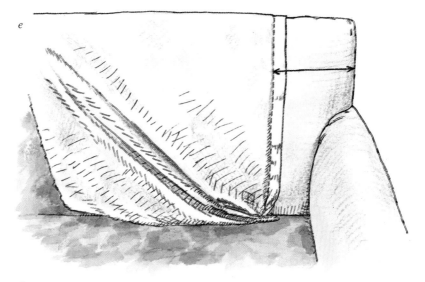

e

f

Arm

g

h

7 With the fabric tucked in, find the point on the top of the arm where the tuck-in disappears. Mark this point on the wrong side of the fabric, and cut downward diagonally almost to the mark (f). Repeat on the other side.

8 Take the fabric around to the side and pin it in place. Form a dart at the top corner and pin it. Trim the edges to 2.5cm/1in; notch (g). Repeat at the other side.

9 Tuck the inside back fabric into the crease by the arm. Insert a pencil, and mark the fabric at the bottom innermost point. Pull out the fabric and trim it to within 5cm/2in of the line. Clip the edge at short intervals (h). Tuck the fabric into the crease.

Inside arm

10 Measure inside arm from point of tuck-in to chosen position of underarm seam on the outside (i). (Seaming the fabric here makes it possible for the pattern to run upward on both sides of arm, and it also results in a better fit.) Add tuck-in and seam allowances. Cut two pieces to this measurement, matching the pattern if necessary.

i

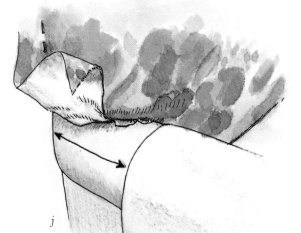

j

k

11 Place the fabric over the arm, leaving enough overhang at the front to accommodate the outward curve of the arm, plus a generous seam allowance. At the back of the arm, fold back the fabric at the point where the inside arm meets the inside back, and measure from the fold to the outside edge (j). Add seam allowance and cut straight down the fabric at this measurement.

12 Fold back the fabric at the front arm scroll. Trim 4cm/1½in back from the fold, following the curve of the scroll (k). On the wrong side of the inside arm, mark the tuck-in point and cut diagonally down nearly to the mark.

13 Pin the inside arm piece to the seat piece at the front. Cut away any excess, and snip into the seam line where necessary on the curve.

14 With a ruler, find the point where the tuck-in finishes at the back of the arm. Fold back the fabric and cut diagonally to this point (l). Tuck in the back edge of the inside arm. Pin the inside back and the arm pieces together along the seam line from the end of the tuck-in to the side edges. If the shape of the sofa requires it, fold and pin darts in the fabric. Trim away excess fabric. The inside back, inside arms, and seat of the sofa have now been fitted (m).

Outside arm
15 Measure the depth of the outside arm from the underarm seam to the skirt seam line (already marked with pins), and add top and bottom seam allowances. Cut two lengths of fabric to this measurement.

16 Pin the fabric to the sofa, allowing 2.5cm/1in at the front, top, and bottom edges. Trim away excess fabric at the back edge, leaving a seam allowance. Pin the inside and outside arm pieces together and notch (n).

Outside back
17 Measure the outside back from seam line down to marked skirt seam line. Add seam allowances, and cut two panels to this measurement. Join them as described for the seat (step 2) but on the right hand side, sew only 5cm/2in down from the top edge to allow for the insertion of the Velcro fastening. (In other cases it may be preferable to position the opening in a corner seam, depending on how the furniture is arranged in the room.)

18 Pin the outside back to the sofa, and pin the edges of the opening together. Then pin the outside back to the inside back and outside arm pieces, notching the edges.

Arm scrolls

19 To facilitate the fitting of arm scrolls, place the sofa on trestles, if possible; otherwise you will have to crouch. Alternatively, tip the sofa onto its back. Pin the outside arm and seat pieces together at the front; notch the edges, and trim excess to 4cm/1½in above this point, following the scroll curves.

20 From spare fabric find two matching pieces, slightly larger than the arm scroll. Measure and cut two rectangles to the required width (at widest point) and depth, plus seam allowances. Pin these to the arm scroll, then to the surrounding edges, keeping the tension firm. Form a dart, if necessary, on the inside arm for a good fit. Notch edges at frequent intervals to facilitate seaming (o).

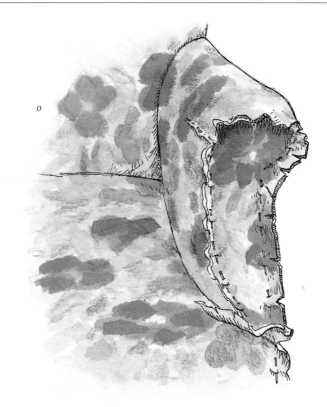

o

Skirt and piping

21 Check the lower edge of the cover to make sure it falls 2.5cm/1in below the marked skirt seamline. Mark and trim it if necessary.

22 Measure the seams to be piped. On this sofa, all exposed seams are piped; so, too, are the top and bottom edges of the cushions.

23 From the remaining fabric, cut the required number of widths for the skirt (in this case, 7, but for other sizes and styles it could be more or fewer), cutting across the whole width of the fabric and making each one 5cm/2in deeper than the required finished depth. Now cut enough bias strips for all the piping (steps 2-3, p168); make the piping (steps 12-13, p169).

24 Unpin and remove cover, match right sides together, first making sure that corresponding edges are notched and replacing the pins along stitching lines of darts. Join all the tuck-ins and continuations of these seams: inside arms to seat edge, inside back to seat back, inside arms to inside back. Stitch all darts.

25 Stitch piping to the outside back along the side and top edges and to the underarm seam edge of outside arm pieces (steps 16-17, p169).

26 Join the outside arms to the inside arms.

27 Join the outside back to inside back, inside arm, and outside arms.

28 Stitch piping around the arm scrolls, starting at the outside arms. Join the arm scrolls to the outside arms, inside arms, and seats, then the outside arms to the seat, enclosing the piping (p).

29 Attach piping to the entire lower edge of the cover, taking care to ease carefully for a good fit.

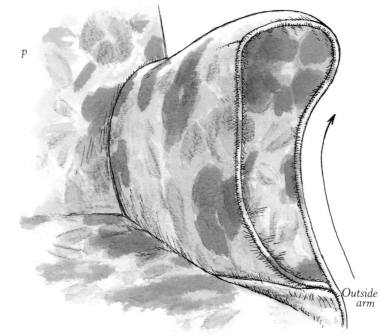

p

Outside arm

178

30 Put the cover on the sofa, then place the cushions on it to mark the positions of the inverted pleats on the skirt. Mark the lower edge of the cover where the cushions meet, then measure to make sure that these points are equidistant from the ends. The pleats will be located at these two points and at the front and back legs, making six in all.

31 Mark the center of the cover and the center of one skirt piece, and pin skirt over cover at that point. At one end, fold the fabric twice to make one half of an inverted pleat, making the folds 5cm/2in deep. Adjust as necessary to align the first fold with the point where the cushions meet. Mark this point (the center of the pleat) on the skirt, then measure off another 7.5cm/ 3in, and cut off excess fabric (q). The seam will thus fall at one of the inner folds of the pleat. Pin the side piece to the center piece, 2.5cm/1in from their edges, and fold the side piece to complete the pleat. Repeat for the other side.

32 Continue pinning the front and side skirt panels to the cover, making inverted pleats at the corners. Conceal the seams, if possible, in the pleats. At the back, cut and pin the skirt so that the seams will coincide with the seams on the outside back. Cut the piece for the right-hand skirt panel to extend 4cm/1½in past the seam line of the cover. Unpin the skirt panels from sofa.

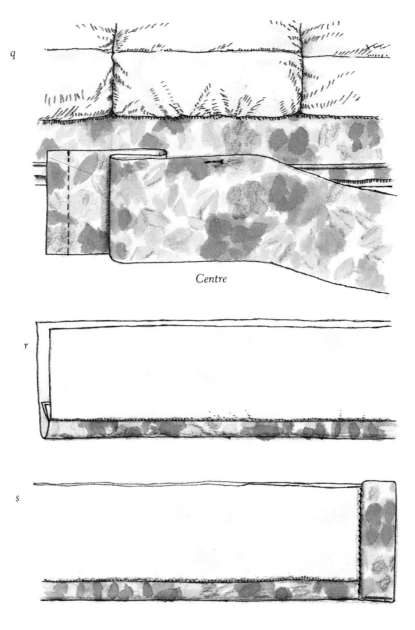

Centre

33 Cut a piece of lining for each skirt panel. Make the lining for the right-hand back panel 6cm/2in shorter than the fabric piece. Join all skirt pieces and all lining pieces along their short sides, in the correct order, matching the pattern. Press seams open.

34 Join skirt to lining along bottom edges, right sides together, taking 1cm/½in seam allowances. Press seam allowances toward lining.

Turn skirt right side out; pull seam up 2.5cm/1in to lining side; press. Trim upper edge of lining even with skirt. Trim lining allowances to reduce bulk (r).

35 Turn under 1cm/½in, then 3cm/1in on right-hand end of skirt. Hem over raw edge of lining (s). Slipstitch lower edges together.

36 Measure the finished depth of skirt from the bottom edge (see

step 1); pin along this line. Join skirt and lining here.

37 Pin the center front of the skirt to the center front of the piped edge of the seat, and re-fit the inverted pleats to either side. Work all around the edge, fitting pleats at corners. Stitch in place.

38 Attach Velcro to the opening edges, including the skirt (steps 24-25, p170).

Top and bottom

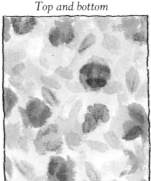

Front border

Side borders

Cushions

39 Begin with the central straight seat and back cushions. Measure the cushion top and add 2.5cm/1in. Cut a paper template and cut a top and bottom piece. Measure the depth of the border and add 2.5cm/1in. Cut one piece across the width of the fabric to this measurement for the front border. Cut two side boxing pieces. Cut a piece for the back boxing (the length of which will extend around each side by the depth of the finished boxing). Cut this 5cm/2in deeper than the others, and cut in half along its length; the zipper will be inserted here.

40 Cut and make piping.

41 Turn under and press 2.5cm/1in on one long edge of each back boxing piece (making sure that these are adjacent edges, so that the pattern runs correctly). Pin (t), baste, and stitch the zipper under each edge in turn, with the fabric edges meeting at the center of the teeth.

t

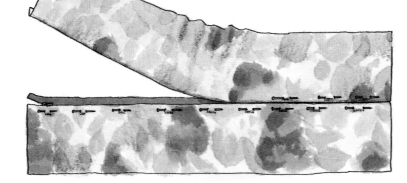

Back boxing

u

42 Mark the center front of the top and bottom pieces. Pin the front boxing to the center of the top cushion piece. If you have to adjust it to match the pattern, trim to fit. Stitch end to side boxing pieces.

43 Attach piping to the top and bottom pieces. Leave about 3cm/1in of piping free at the beginning. When you return to this point, end the stitching about 3cm/1in before reaching the free end of the piping. Cut the finishing end so that it overlaps the starting end by 3cm/1in, and unpick the stitches on the piping itself for a short distance. Turn under 1.5cm/½in of the piping fabric.Cut the finishing end of the piping cord so that it just meets the starting end (u). Butt the two ends together and enclose the starting end with the unpicked fabric. Continue the line of stitching to complete the piped edge.

44 Find the center back of the top and of the back boxing, and pin and stitch, leaving just over 2.5cm/1in unstitched at each end. Similarly, pin front and side strips to the front and sides of the top; trim side strips to fit where they meet the back boxing, and pin the edges together (v). Stitch the side and back strips. Stitch around the remaining edge, turning the zipper tape to the sides, so it lies flat (w).

v

w

45 To join the bottom panel, first mark the corners of the boxing edges. To do this, follow a thread from the stitched corner up to the raw edge, marking it with chalk or pencil as you go, and notch the edge at that point. Repeat on remaining corners. Open the zipper. Pin the bottom panel to the boxing, matching the corners (x), and stitch it in place. Finish the edges by machine to prevent fraying. Turn the cover right side out.

Bottom

x

Shaped cushions

46 These are made in essentially the same way as the straight cushions. However, remember when cutting out the top and bottom that a left and a right will be required for each and that the pattern must run correctly; label the pieces to avoid confusion. The zipper is inserted in the bottom boxing strip of the inside back cushions (y) and to the back boxing of the seat cushions. Special care is required to ensure that the piping follows the edges accurately; clip at short intervals.

Bottom border

y

Glossary of Terms

Base burlap A layer of burlap placed over the webbing and/or springs to support the pad.

Bias cutting Cutting fabric diagonally across the weave.

Bottom lining A piece of fabric tacked to the underside of a chair. Also called a dustcatcher.

Bridle ties Loops of twine that hold stuffing in place.

Buttoning A method of producing hollows in the upholstery pad with carefully positioned buttons.

Close nailing Decorative nails inserted close together along the edge of the top cover.

Deck A seat having a raised front edge and a slightly lower main section, fitted with a cushion.

Dished seat A seat shaped with a slight hollow in the center. Also called a saddle seat.

Double-stuffed pad A pad that has two stuffings: the first is secured by scrim and stuffing ties; the second is covered with muslin.

Edge roll A firmly stuffed curved edge on an upholstery pad, now achieved partly with stitching.

Edwardian Dating from the reign of Edward VII of England (1901–1910).

Finger-roll edge A small edge roll.

Fly An extension piece, made of inexpensive fabric, stitched to the top cover where it will not be seen.

Gimp A flat braid used to conceal the edge of the top cover.

Lashing The lacing and knotting together of coil springs.

Lumbar roll A curved shape given to the inside back of a chair.

Pad The layers of burlap, stuffing, and other soft materials that form the cushioning of upholstery. Also sometimes called the "cake."

Pin stuffing A flat, single stuffing with a shallow edge.

Piping Fabric-covered cord inserted in the seam of a top cover or slipcover for decoration. Also called welting or cording.

Pleated tufting A method of buttoning or tufting that produces a pad defined by deep folds and accentuated by tiny buttons.

Regulate To adjust the stuffing within a pad.

Renaissance revival A style of furniture popular in the late 1800s, characterized by a return to straighter lines and classical motifs.

Rococo revival A mid-19th-century style of furnishings reminiscent of 18th-century rococo.

Second stuffing See Double-stuffed pad.

Selvage Extra-firmly woven edge of fabric which will not ravel.

Show wood The visible part of a chair frame, polished and often decoratively carved.

Spring ties Stitches worked over springs, using twine, to secure them to the webbing and the base burlap.

Sprung edge A flexible edge for a seat, formed by a separate row of springs worked on the front rail.

Squab A flat, tightly stuffed cushion, sometimes with box sides.

Star buttoning A soft, informal style of buttoning popular in the mid-19th century.

Stitched edge The stitching on the edge of a pad which gives it strength and defines shape.

Stuffing ties Long running stitches which help to keep the first stuffing in position. When pulled tight they flatten and firm the pad, preparing it for the top stuffing. Also called quilting stitches.

Tack hold A method of fastening twine or cord to a rail by knotting or twisting it around a tack, and then tacking off, to secure it.

Tack off To drive a tack fully home into the rail.

Tack roll A variety of finger-roll edge in which the scrim for the roll is tacked to the rail, rather than stitched.

Tack ties The tension lines created in a fabric when it has been tacked too tightly, or with the threads misaligned.

Taking down The stripping of existing covering and/or stuffing and other materials from the frame.

Temporary tack To drive a tack halfway into the frame to allow for removal and/or re-positioning of materials. Also called baste tacking or slip tacking.

Tufting A pattern of shallow indentations in a pad; similar to buttoning, but with small clumps of threads at the tied points.

Webbing Strong woven fabric strips, made of linen, burlap, or canvas, fixed to the base of a chair or sofa to support the upholstery. Also the pattern thus formed.

Suppliers

Jacket
Fabric: Bird and Basket
(Bennison Fabrics)
Dried flowers: Chattels, 53 Chalk
Farm Road, London NW1

Page 8
Chintz: Hadleigh (Titley & Marr)

Pages 51, 53, 55
Tools and materials: The Easy
Chair Upholstery Centre

Pages 46-47
Fabric: Walsingham (The
Gainsborough Silk Weaving Co)

Page 57
1 Quadrille (H. A. Percheron),
2 Chastleton (Stuart Renaissance
Textiles), **3** Walsingham (Stuart
Renaissance Textiles), **4** Ludlow
(Laura Ashley), **5** Damas Fleuri

"Forest" (Designers Guild), **6** Albert
(Laura Ashley), **7** India Stripe
(Bennison Fabrics), **8** Bellini
(Sahco-Hesslein), **9** The Hoopoo
(Gainsborough Silk Weaving
Company), **10** Verona
(Blendworth), **11** Savoy (Sahco-
Hesslein), **12** Egypt (Stuart
Renaissance Textiles).

Page 59
1 Baskets (Karl's), **2** Little Chelsea
(Sanderson), **3** Kensington Bows
(Titley & Marr), **4** Venezia
Cherubino (Warner Fabrics),
5 Vermont (Marvic Textiles),
6 Emma (Laura Ashley), **7** Letizia
(Marvic Textiles), **8** Vernantes
(Pierre Frey), **9** Mirabel (Robert
Allen Fabrics), **10** Country Lattice
(Laura Ashley), **11** La Salle Ribbon
Damask (Warner Fabrics),
12 Pompadour (Marvic Textiles).

Page 61
1 Sunstitch (Osborne & Little),
2 Shiraz (Marvic Textiles),
3 Venezia Carnevale (Warner
Fabrics), **4** Anatolia (Osborne &
Little), **5** Patiné (Osborne & Little),
6 Octagon (Bennison Fabrics),
7 Merina (Osborne & Little),
8 Tideway (Jamasque), **9** Kate
(Busby and Busby), **10** Chervough
(Sahco-Hesslein), **11** Marisol
(Robert Allen Fabrics), **12** Lusso
(Christian Fischbacher).

Page 63
Trimmings: Wemyss-Houlès
Limited, 40 Newman Street,
London W1P 3PA

Slip Seat (page 117)
Covered in Faded Green Oakleaf
(Bennison Fabrics)
Alternative fabrics:
1 Rayol (Sahco-Hesslein)
2 Horsehair Rep (John Boyd
Textiles)
3 Striped Misa Moiré (Marvic
Textiles)
4 Medici (Sahco-Hesslein)

Page 117

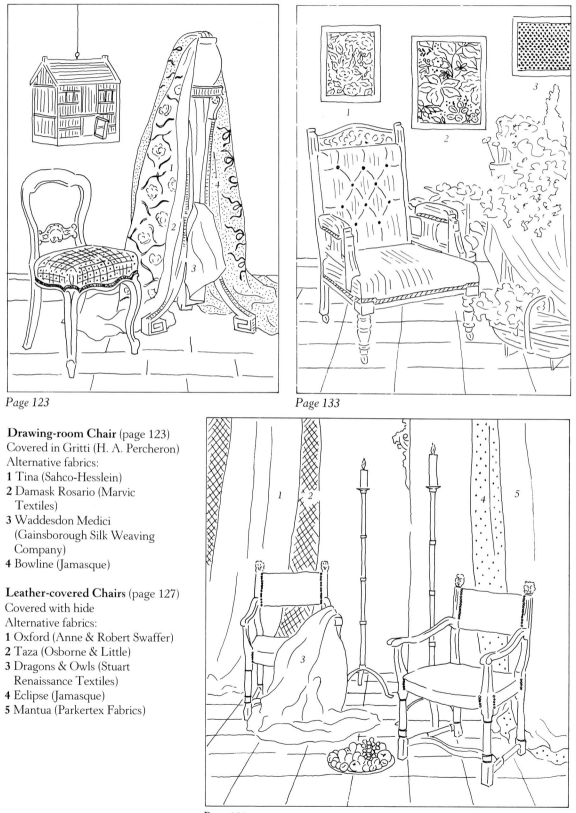

Page 123

Page 133

Drawing-room Chair (page 123)
Covered in Gritti (H. A. Percheron)
Alternative fabrics:
1 Tina (Sahco-Hesslein)
2 Damask Rosario (Marvic Textiles)
3 Waddesdon Medici (Gainsborough Silk Weaving Company)
4 Bowline (Jamasque)

Leather-covered Chairs (page 127)
Covered with hide
Alternative fabrics:
1 Oxford (Anne & Robert Swaffer)
2 Taza (Osborne & Little)
3 Dragons & Owls (Stuart Renaissance Textiles)
4 Eclipse (Jamasque)
5 Mantua (Parkertex Fabrics)

Page 127

Late Victorian Armchair (page 133)
Covered in black and white
mattress ticking
Alternative fabrics:
1 Grimaldi (Sahco-Hesslein)
2 Wheatflower (Bennison Fabrics)
3 The Kingsley (Gainsborough Silk
   Weaving Company)

Iron-framed Armchair
(page 138)
Covered in Bird and Basket
(Bennison Fabrics)
Alternative fabrics:
1 Lacewing (Jamasque)
2 Herb Robert (Laura Ashley)
3 Moiré Exotique (H. A.
   Percheron)
4 Damask Old Rose (Designers
   Guild)

Page 138

Chaise Longue (page 146)
Covered in gold damask and a
contrasting solid-color fabric
Alternative fabrics:
1 Damas Josephine (H. A.
   Percheron)
2 Coutil Stripe (Jamasque)
3 Arezzo (Sahco-Hesslein)
4 Toile de Jouy La Bastille (H. A.
   Percheron)

Page 146

Wing Chair (page 153)
Covered in Montrose (Boozac of France)
Alternative fabrics:
1 Medici (Sahco-Hesslein)
2 Wembley (Parkertex Fabrics)
3 Rosetti (Jamasque)
4 Malmaison (Osborne & Little)
5 Victoria (Sahco-Hesslein)

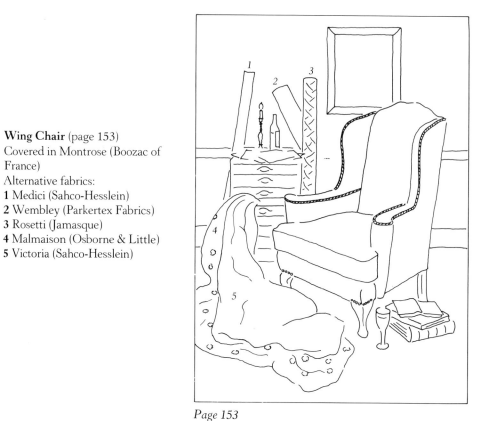

Page 153

Chesterfield (page 160)
Covered in Hayderabad (Manuel Canovas)
Alternative fabrics:
1 Faded Roses (Bennison Fabrics)
2 Savoy (Sahco-Hesslein)
3 Safi (Osborne & Little)
4 Jacquard Florence (H. A. Percheron)

Page 160

Breakfast-room Chairs (page 167)
Covered in gingham fabric (Ian
Mankin) and floral printed cotton
Alternative fabrics:
1 Percale "Les Clochettes" (H.A.
 Percheron)
2 Kammaren (Karl's)
3 Iris (Karl's)
4 Toile de Jouy
Dishes lent by Laura Ashley

Page 167

Three-seater Sofa (page 172)
Covered in Giardino (Designers
Guild)
Alternative fabrics:
1 Belinda (Sahco-Hesslein)
2 Moiré Mandarin (H. A.
 Percheron)
3 Blueberry (Laura Ashley)
4 Cotton Chintz (Laura Ashley)

Page 172

Useful Addresses

Upholstery Supplies
For retailers of upholstery supplies in your area, consult the Yellow Pages, or contact one of the following:

J & J Supplies, Inc.
114 Eldridge Street
New York, NY 10002
(212) 431 1115

Greentex Upholstery Supplies
236 West 26th Street
New York, NY 10001
(212) 206 8585

Active Foam Products
629 West Cermak Road
Chicago, IL 60616
(312) 666 2116

Dubois Fabrics and Upholstery Supplies
5520 West 111th Street
Oaklawn, IL 60453
(312) 499 2040

Mid-States Upholstery Supply Co.
3041 West Lawrence Avenue
Chicago, IL 60625
(312) 463 1680

Cushion Works
3320 18th Street
San Francisco, CA 94110
(415) 552 6220

Suppliers of fabrics used in the projects

Bennison Fabrics Ltd.
Mail Order available from:
16 Holbein Place
London SW1 8N7
United Kingdom

John Boyd Textiles Ltd.
Contact:
Scalamandré Silks Inc.
300 Trade Zone Drive
Ronkonkoma, NY 11779
(516) 467 8800

Boozac of France
4700 33rd Street
Long Island City
NY 11101
(718) 482 7866

Manuel Canovas Inc.
Stockists nationwide
Head office:
D & D Building
979 Third Avenue
New York NY 10022
(212) 752 9588

Designers Guild
Branches nationwide
Main stockist:
Osborne & Little
D & D Building
Suite 1503N
979 Third Avenue
New York NY 10022
(212) 752 2890

The Gainsborough Silk Weaving Co. Ltd.
Agent:
R. Hugh Gardener
P.O. Box 103
Murray Hill Station
New York NY 10156
(212) 532 6418

Jamasque
Kirk-Brummel Associates
826 Broadway
New York NY 10003
(212) 477 8580

Laura Ashley
Branches nationwide
Head office:
(201) 934 3000

Marvic Textiles
Clarence House
211 E. 58th Street
New York
NY 10022
(212) 752 2890

Osborne & Little P.L.C.
65 Commerce Road
Stamford CT 06902
(203) 335 9510

Parkertex Fabrics
Distributors:
Brunschwig et Fils
75 Virginia Road
North White Plains NY 10603
(914) 684 5800

H.A. Percheron Ltd.
Agents:
Brunschwig et Fils
(address above)

Clarence House
(address above)

Sahco-Hesslein Ltd
Head office:
Bergamo Fabrics
37-20 34th Street
Long Island City NY 11101
(718) 392 5000

Stuart Renaissance Textiles
Agents:
Classic Revivals Inc.
1 Design Center Place
Suite 545
Boston MA 02201
(617) 574 9030

Anne & Robert Swaffer
Stockists:
Jaynor Furnishing Inc.
P.O. Box 1035
3907 Nancy Lane
Seaford NY 11783
(516) 783 7373

Titley & Marr
Agents:
Cowtan and Tout, Inc.
979 Third Avenue
New York NY 10022
(212) 753 4488

Index

Editor Susanne Haines   **Design and research** Anne Wilson
Editorial assistants Barbara Vesey, Diana Loxley
Production control Georgina McNamara
Editorial Director Erica Hunningher   **Art Director** Caroline Hillier

Author's acknowledgments

My editor, Susanne Haines, and my designer, Anne
Wilson, have worked with me as a united team, and to
them both I would like to express my very deep thanks
for giving so unstintingly of their energy, expertise,
and, so importantly, their enthusiasm. Indeed, Frances
Lincoln and her staff always help and encourage,
including Katy Foskew whose cheery voice on the
telephone brightens the dullest day. I would like to
thank Susan Berry for initiating this project.

Philip, my business partner, whose workshop always
runs to an overtight schedule, cleared the way on
numerous occasions for project deadlines to be met and
carried unquestioningly the extra work load that my
preoccupation with this book necessitated. Debbie,
Simon, and Bernard are the hands in this book and
patiently worked and re-worked, becoming as good at
camera angles as they are at stuffing and stitching.
Joyce French, whom I always turn to when asked to
produce slipcovers, demonstrated her craftsmanship to
me with clarity. Jim Robins has produced illustrations
that show, not only accurately, but beautifully, how to
follow my instructions. Tim Imrie, together with Anne,
has captured the spirit of the chairs and sofas in his
photographs. Dizzy and Gulliver, knowing nothing and
caring less about upholstery or books, wagged their
tails and kept it all in perspective. And of course there
is Richard, whose support is total. I thank them all for
contributing so much so generously in so many ways.

Publishers' acknowledgments

The publishers would like to thank the following
individuals for their help in producing this book. Tim
Imrie for his photography; Jim Robins for his
illustrations; Joyce French for the slipcover projects;
Edward Cooke, Jr., of the Museum of Fine Arts,
Boston, for help in preparing the American edition,
and for historical consultation; Jacqui Hurst; Tig
Sutton; Eleanor Van Zandt for editing the American
edition; Penny David; Vicky Hayward; Emma Callery;
Vicki Robinson.

The publishers would like to thank the following
companies. For the loan of upholstery materials: The
Easy Chair Upholstery Centre. For the loan and/or
supply of fabrics and trimmings: Bennison Fabrics
Ltd., Blendworth, John Boyd Textiles Ltd., Brooke
Fairbairn & Co., Busby & Busby, Christian
Fischbacher, Pierre Frey, Manuel Canovas, Designers
Guild, The Gainsborough Silk Weaving Co. Ltd.,
Jamasque, Karl's, Laura Ashley, Marvic Textiles,
Osborne & Little P.L.C., Parkertex Fabrics Ltd., H.A.
Percheron Ltd., Sahco-Hesslein U.K. Ltd., Sanderson,
Stuart Renaissance Textiles, Anne & Robert Swaffer,
Titley & Marr, Warner Fabrics, Wemyss-Houlès. For
the loan of props for photography: Chattels, Davies,
The Garden Centre at Alexandra Palace, Raffles,
Waterhouse & Dodd.

Illustration and photographic acknowledgments

All illustrations by Jim Robins, except
pp166-181 by Tig Sutton.

All special photography by Tim
Imrie, except p6 by Jacqui Hurst.
Photographs © Frances Lincoln Limited.

For permission to reproduce the
paintings, engravings and photographs
in this book, the publishers thank:
Alte Pinakothek, Munich: p32;
Bibliothèque Nationale, Paris: *Femme
de qualité déshabillé pour le bain*, 1685,
p22; Bridgeman Art Library, London
(by kind permission of the Dowager
Marchioness of Cholmondeley) pp12-
13; (Wellington Museum, Apsley
House, London) p21; (Musée du
Louvre, Paris) p33; (Tate Gallery,
London) p43; Chatto and Windus

Publishers: p36; Country Life Picture
Library: p35; Mary Evans Picture
Library: p4, p27, p30; Harvard
University Portrait Collection, Fogg
Art Museum, Cambridge,
Massachusetts (Bequest of Ward
Nicholas Boylston in 1828) p29;
Leighton House Museum, London:
p39; Richard Moore: p45; Museo
Civico di Torino: p42; The National
Gallery, London: p17; *Madame de
Pompadour* (detail), 1763, p25; the
National Gallery of Art, Washington
(Collection of Mr. and Mrs. Paul
Mellon) p40; the National Portrait
Gallery, London: p16; National Trust
Photographic Library, Dyrham Park:
p18; Victoria & Albert Museum,

London (Courtesy of the Board of
Trustees) p10; p11; *Dame de la plus
haute qualité* (detail), (left), and *Femme
de qualité en déshabillé négligé* (detail),
(right), p23; p24; p28; *The Cabinet
Maker, Upholsterer and General Artist's
Encyclopaedia*, c. 1660s, p31; from
Ackerman's Repository, 1810, p34; from
the *Journal für Tapezierer und
Dekorateure*, 1871, by Carl Hettwig,
p37; *Sammlung Moderner Sitzmöbel für
alle Räume des Hauses*, p41; *Decorative
Draperies and Upholstery*, 1937, by
Henry W. Frohne, p44; The Wallace
Collection, London (reproduced by
kind permission of the Trustees): p14;
p19; p26; Worcester Art Museum,
Worcester, Massachusetts: p20.